Bojagi is a traditional Korean textile art technique. Centuries old, the bojagi (wrapping cloths) were originally made for everyday living with scraps of leftover fabrics artfully put together, resembling the colourful and luminous works of modern artists such as Piet Mondrian and Paul Klee.

Leading expert Sara Cook's simple and easy-to-follow introduction to the art form demonstrates each of the traditional techniques, and explores how modern textile artists and quilters can interpret the principles of bojagi in creative and exciting new ways.

Beginning with a simple guide to the different types of bojagi, Sara's historical and cultural introduction goes on to describe the Eastern aesthetic principles behind the work and the symbolism of the colours and designs found throughout Korean art, architecture and textiles.

She covers all the fabrics (ramie, hemp and silk) and sewing equipment needed, before going on to demonstrate, with step-by-step diagrams and contemporary examples, each of the seams – *garumsol*, *tongsol*, *ssamsol* and *kkekki* – and each of the embellishments – *bakgi mae dup*, *dutlam sangchim* and *setlam sangchim*, *jat ssi* and *kileoki* – found in traditional bojagi. She then goes on to show how these can be used to spectacular effect in the different forms of *jogakbo* (pieced patchwork) as well as demonstrating the intricate art of *saeksil nubi* (coloured-thread quilting).

With a foreword from internationally renowned bojagi practitioner Chunghie Lee, alongside contributions from other international artists, this beautiful and inspirational book offers textile artists and quilters a range of ideas to create their own stunning forms of bojagi.

Bojagi

Sara Cook

Bojagi

DESIGN AND TECHNIQUES IN
KOREAN TEXTILE ART

BATSFORD

First published in the United Kingdom in 2019 by Batsford
43 Great Ormond Street
London WC1N 3HZ

An imprint of B. T. Batsford Holdings Limited

ISBN: 9781849945219

A CIP catalogue record for this book is available from
the British Library.

27 26 25 24
10 9 8 7 6 5 4 3 2

Reproduction by Colour Depth, UK
Printed by Toppan Leefung Printing Ltd, China

This book can be ordered direct from the publisher at
www.batsfordbooks.com, or try your local bookshop.

Distributed in the United States and Canada by
Sterling Publishing Co., Inc.
1166 Avenue of the Americas,
17th Floor, New York, NY 10036

Contents

Bojagi and Beyond

My own story with bojagi began when I saw 'Stitch by Stitch: No-Name Woman Works', a bojagi exhibit curated by Dr Huh Dong-hwa at the The National Folk Museum of Korea in 1983. The high aesthetic composition and use of colour in an ordinary bojagi shocked the nation – and sparked my use of the technique as a modern textile artist.

In 1994, I had the honour to be an exchange visiting faculty member (from Hongik University in Seoul) at the Rhode Island School of Design (RISD), a prominent fine arts and design college in the US. Numerous opportunities of introducing bojagi to many parts of the world followed, and subsequently, from 1999 through 2017, I taught the course 'Bojagi and Beyond' at RISD. This class was made available to students of all majors, from first-year college students to postgraduates, and so the traditional Korean woman's living room was being reinterpreted by students with fresh minds, unclouded by stereotypes.

I wanted to share the astonishing reinterpretations of bojagi that emerged during classes, and so began introducing the curated works of RISD students at the Daegu International Textile Fair. In addition, I continued to review the reinterpretations made by textile artists of various countries and curated four exhibits to represent Korea as the Guest of Honour Nation at the 2010 European Patchwork Meeting in France. From this the International Korea Bojagi Forum was conceived, and it began in 2012. It is held every two years, comprised of an exhibition, lectures, workshops and a cultural tour. The goal is to globalize bojagi, to cultivate international friendship, and to promote the design of bojagi while inspiring people to work with their hands. It is becoming a place for many international artists, writers and textile enthusiasts to gather and interact in Korea, the motherland of bojagi.

I met Sara Cook when she came to the Korea Bojagi Forum held in Suwon in 2016. She was not merely attending the daily events of the forum; rather, she was passionate about gaining in-depth knowledge of bojagi by participating in workshops such as *chogakbo* (patched bojagi) by one of the bojagi masters Jung Hee Na and Korean traditional dyeing specialist Hyehong Chang. Thereafter, she continued to attend bojagi classes in the US taught by Youngmin Lee.

I realized Sara's works were unusual and original and invited her to participate in the 2018 International Forum as a practising artist representing the UK, among six specially invited international bojagi artists who were to have individual exhibitions. (The other five artists were from Finland, US, France, Japan and the Netherlands). Sara's piece, *Greyline*, was beyond technical perfection and demonstrated an outstanding aesthetic sense. She works on a large scale using colour contrast and dimensional surface treatments, making a two-dimensional work appear to be three dimensional. She also demonstrates a great analytical ability through the execution of her series of small works.

Sara's display at the International Forum was well thought out and beautifully designed and hung. In addition to her large works, she also presented a collection of small works that clearly showed her to be not just as an artist, but an educator. Currently, as the Director of the Brighton Fashion and Textile School, she is in a position to teach a broad range of students and share her expertise in various textile techniques. In this role, she is not merely passing on the techniques of making bojagi, she is able to instruct students to freely reinterpret and express themselves by combining bojagi methods with various other techniques. As such, she is outstandingly well qualified to publish a book about bojagi in the UK. I congratulate her and very much look forward to the great results of her teachings and her published work on bojagi.

CHUNGHIE LEE
www.koreabojagiforum.com

Introduction

I first became interested in bojagi when I saw the contemporary exhibition *My Cup Overflows* by Chunghie Lee at the 2009 Festival of Quilts in Birmingham. I was both intrigued by the construction and captivated by the use of transparency. Lee's work was inspired by all those unknown women who had made beautiful wrapping cloths that are collectively known as bojagi. This led me to start researching Korean wrapping cloths and has given me opportunities to travel and subsequently exhibit my own work both in the UK and in Korea.

Invitations by Chunghie Lee to attend the Korea Bojagi Forums in 2016 and 2018 introduced me to many exciting new textile artists who have been inspired by the principles of bojagi in their work. They have also given me the opportunity to work with teachers and to study museum collections in South Korea.

Researching bojagi has inspired me to experiment with the traditional narrow seams, creating irregular grids. When this is combined with transparency in the fabric the seaming structure creates a further linear dimension. This is often revealed in the shadows that the seams cast and has enabled me to evoke the feeling of light moving across the landscape in recent work like *Greyline*.

For centuries textiles were one of the few ways Korean women could express their creativity. The designs and symbolism in bojagi now inspire many textile artists around the world. You will see how bojagi have been reinterpreted in many different types of two- and three-dimensional media.

This book is the culmination of ten years of research into historic practitioners and artists today, those based in Korea and those practising across the world. In putting this book together, I hope to share this knowledge so that even more people can be inspired by the ancient traditions whose designs can still spark design innovation for the modern textile artist today.

Greyline #3 *showing* khojipgi *(pinching technique) on two layers of organdie, silk, thread and dye paint. See page 86 for more on* khojipgi.

The "grey line" is the boundary between night and day
Propagation along the grey line is very efficient. One major reason for this is that the D
layer
radio
"회색
라디오
청취지
장거리 통신을 하실 수 있습니다

The "grey line" is the boundary between night and day
Propagation along the grey line is very efficient. One major reason for this is that the D
layer
radio
"회색
라디오
청취지
장거리 통신을 하실 수 있습니다

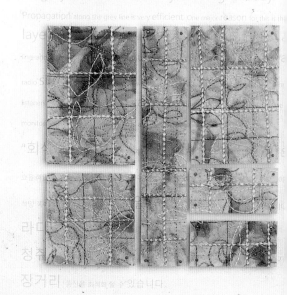

The "grey line" is the boundary between night and day
Propagation along the grey line is very efficient. One major reason for this is that the D
layer
wave
radio
"회
라디오
청
장거리 통신을 하실 수 있습니다

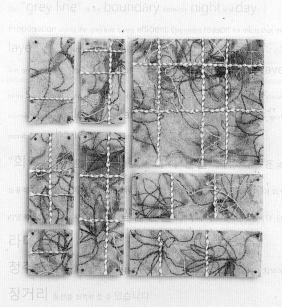

The "grey line" is the boundary between night and day. The line that divides night and day, the daylight map. The grey line travels around the world like a silent wave, never ending, ruled by the turn of the planet moving around the sun. The time when dreams and flashes of inspiration are at their strongest in that hazy time between waking and sleeping. It's the time when shortwave radio signals travel around the world the quickest. Ham radio operators and shortwave listeners can optimize long distance communications to various areas of the world monitoring this band as it moves around the globe.

The "grey line" is the boundary between night and day
Propagation along the grey line is very efficient. One major reason for this is that the D
layer
wave
radio sign
listeners can
monitoring the band
"회색
라디오
청취지
장거리 통신을 하실 수 있습니다

The "grey line" is the boundary between night and day
Propagation along the grey line is very efficient. One major reason for this is that the D
layer
wa
radio S
listeni
monitor
"회색
라디오
청취지
장거리 통신을 하실 수 있습니다

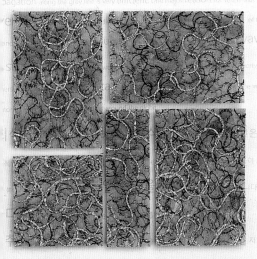

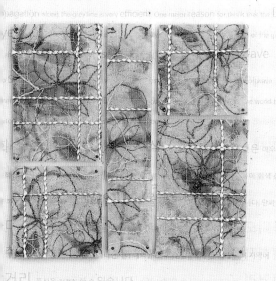

Greyline #2, *made from fabric trimmed away from the French seams in the piece* Greyline #1 *(see pages 106–107).* Silk organza, water-soluble fabrics *and free-machine embroidery. It is part of Korean tradition to use every scrap of fabric, even trimmings from other pieces.*

CHAPTER 1

HISTORY AND
CULTURAL
INFLUENCES

Earliest surviving examples of bojagi

Bojagi (formerly romanized as *pojagi*) translates as wrapping cloth and is the over-arching name given to this type of stitched textile. Most of the surviving examples of bojagi date to the Joseon Dynasty (1392–1897) but some can be dated as far back as the Three Kingdoms period (57BC–668AD). The earliest surviving bojagi dates from 1055–1101 and was used as a table covering for the eminent Buddhist priest, Taegak Kuksa Uich'on and can be found in Son'am-sa monastery in Sungju, South Jeolla province.

According to a survey by Han Sangsu on the studies of Korean embroidery, early examples from the Joseon dynasty are the seven wrapping cloths made by Lady Yi in 1415. They were made to cover the Buddhist scriptures that her husband, Yu Kon, had copied. Three of the wrapping cloths are decorated with embroidered images of lotus flowers, grasses, cranes, clouds and tang scrolls. These are now held in the collection of the Jeonju National Museum.

Dosan Seowon Confucian temple, Andong, Korea.

The earliest surviving example of a wrapping cloth used in the royal household of the Joseon Dynasty is made of dark blue silk with a cloud pattern and the seven treasures design. It is lined in plain blue silk and measures three *pok* – approximately 105cm (41in) square. It belonged to Princess Myongan and was made to wrap her ceremonial wedding items in 1681. This piece was formerly part of the Museum of Korean Embroidery's collection of *kungbo* (royal court) bojagi textiles and is in the process of being catalogued before being displayed in one of Seoul's new museums.

Wrapping cloth for wrapping a gift. Two layers of sukgosa (fine silk gauze), hand stitched.

Gongdan (silk satin) and silk thread wrapping cloth for a wedding letter. Auspicious embroidered images of a peony and butterfly signify good luck and longevity.

The role of bojagi in
Korean culture

Bojagi have played an important role in traditional Korean culture and have been used in the everyday to wrap, carry and store objects. Until the 1950s they were used to wrap or cover everything from bedding and clothes to food dishes and also for religious rituals. These functional domestic items were not made as a hobby but were produced along with clothing and bedding items essential in the household. They were an integral part of daily living, and bojagi remains, as Chunghie Lee has pointed out, 'the living tradition' (hence the name of the 2016 Korea Bojagi Forum: The Living Tradition). Some were pieced together using geometric designs in colourful compositions using leftover household fabrics, whereas others were made from single pieces of cloth and still others were heavily embroidered.

They were nearly all square and around one to ten *pok* – 35cm–3.5m (14–11ft 6in) – in size, depending on their use. Some had long ties attached to their corners while others were lined with oiled paper for food coverings with folded-fabric knots used as handles. They served a practical need, were beautifully made and often imbued with symbols for good luck, health and wealth and they seem to have had significance for the maker beyond their practical use. A wrapping cloth can take a simple form but convey a profound message by the use of colour and symbolism.

Used by the rich and poor alike, they could be folded and stored, taking up minimal space in more compact homes. Their uses can give us a glimpse into past lifestyles and ritual practice.

In a middling household, for example, the living space often doubled up as a sleeping area at night as well as a place to eat. Quilted sleeping mats would be folded away and wrapped. Wardrobes and chests of drawers were not common, so clothing and special items were contained and protected by wrapping cloths.

During the Choson period, Confucian philosophy gradually dominated state ideology and impacted on women's social status, so that by the 16th century women's lives were mostly confined to the role of wives. In wealthy and middle-class homes, men and women occupied separate living quarters in the home, with the kitchen in the women's quarters. Women were excluded from any formal education and lived very restricted lives. One way they could express themselves creatively was in making bojagi. This isolation seems to have contributed to the unique work created by these women. No records or images survive of patterns being followed, although there are some surviving Joseon Dynasty court records listing vast numbers of bojagi used and needed for various ceremonial functions.

Winter by Youngmin Lee. Pieced by hand using a ssamsol seam.

Different types of bojagi

Bojagi can be made up from just one layer of pieced fabric or two. A pieced panel could be lined with a single layer of fabric or it could consist of two pieced layers of a different arrangement. Typically bojagi made from cotton, hemp or ramie are of one layer while those made in silk fabrics have one or two layers. Where there are two layers of fabric they are joined together with decorative stitches or a small decorative *bakgi mae dup* or bat knot, a symbolic shape signifying good fortune. The joining of the layers is a practical consideration and is not an equivalent to quilting which was a separate type of bojagi known as *nubi*. A wrapping cloth can have many names according to its style and use, so for example a lined wrapping cloth designed to cover a food table could be a *gyeopbo*, *jogakbo* (patchwork wrapping cloth) or *sang bo* (food-covering cloth).

Gung-bo were bojagi made for the royal family and the palace (*gung* means palace). Court records written at the end of the Choson period have survived and describe the type of cloth and colours that were used: silk fabrics in bright pink, red and paler pinks as well ramie, cotton and hemp.

Min-bo is the name given to bojagi made by ordinary people – those outside the court (known as *yangban*), as well as educated middle-class people but excluding the poor – and these often had more abstract designs (*min* means people).

Gyeopbo means double or lined bojagi and these were made with two pieces of contrasting cloth, one side of which could be plain, while the other could be patterned, embroidered or painted.

Hot-bo means 'single' and is an unlined bojagi used for wrapping and storing daily items such as blankets.

Jasu-bo are embroidered wrapping cloths and were made for weddings and betrothals. They were nearly always lined with a silk fabric while the embroidery was worked onto a cotton background using silk threads. The patterns were first drawn or printed onto thick hanji paper. This was then placed on top of the fabric and the design stitched through both layers. The paper remained in the design, adding extra padding, and the excess fell away as the needle perforated the edges of the shapes. Blue, green, pink, orange, yellow, black and white were the dominant colours used.

Trees feature in the foundation myth of Korea and there are many surviving embroidered bojagi that make use of the idea of a tree in their design. The patterns were flattened and simplified so that the view is aerial. Rainbow-coloured, leafy tree branches spread out, usually from a central point, filling the square frame where leaves become birds with the maker's imagination seemingly running free. These designs are unique to Korea, and

Bojagi wrapping cloth (c.1900). Cotton and silk with embroidery showing a Tree of Life pattern with goose motif.

the symbols used in them were meant to wish the recipient happiness and prosperity in married life.

Embroidery has a long history in Korea and while no extant examples have survived, wall paintings and records indicate its use as early as the Three Kingdoms period (57BC–668AD). According to one account, 'On an auspicious day in early May, officials held a morning meeting. They wore purple clothes with wide sleeves over blue trousers. Their hats were decorated with birds and flowers embroidered in gold' (*100 Thimbles in a Box*, see page 124). During the Goryeo Dynasty (918–1392), whose kingdom gave name to the modern pronunciation 'Korea', girls as young as ten years old were apprenticed to the royal palace *subang*, or embroidery workshop, where all the objects needed for the royal household were made.

Jogaksu-bo is the name for embroidered bojagi, with *su* meaning embroidery. These were most often pieced from regular geometric shapes such as squares and triangles and embroidered with symbolic images such as cranes and lettering – all signifying good luck and happiness.

Jogakbo is the name for bojagi made from small scraps, recycling leftover bits of fabric into abstract patchwork designs, and used to wrap ritual and everyday objects. *Jogak* means small pieces. *Jogakbo* are often likened by academics to modern abstract art such as that created by Mondrian and Klee. Plain fabrics are used to create bold designs with the best

examples demonstrating a perfectly balanced use of colour.

Sikji-bo are oiled paper covering cloths used for food. Bojagi made entirely of oiled paper were made in square and rectangular shapes. They were made from hanji, which is a traditional paper developed in the 4th to 7th centuries AD. Hanji is made from the inner bark of paper mulberry, a tree native to Korea that grows on the rocky mountainsides, and it can be made into lots of different thicknesses, It has a strong, fibrous appearance. It was used to line the walls, floors and lattice windows of the traditional wooden Korean houses, among other uses.

The hanji was treated with soya oil (which stained it a yellow colour). This made the paper food covering cloths easier to wipe clean. The square ones, usually one *pok*, 35cm (14in), in size with a long tie handle, were used to wrap a small amount of food for a journey. The rectangular ones had folded edges to fit over the small low food tables and trays. These paper bojagi were decorated with contrasting black and red oiled cut-paper designs with butterfly wings in the corners and various motifs symmetrically arranged such as bats, floral or geometric shapes. They usually had a plaited handle made of paper.

Remnants of Memory by Youngmin Lee. Bojagi hand stitched with homjil seams, made from cotton fabrics found in an antique market in Seoul, Korea.

Luminous #1 *by Youngmin Lee. Jewel pattern made from* sukgosa *(fine silk gauze). The lining has been used to create a border, which is held in place with* settam sangchim *(three-stitch pattern).*

Sang bo Is the name used to describe bojagi made to cover a food. These could be made from oiled paper or fabric that was lined with oiled paper.

Yeouijumunbo means jewel pattern. This design is well known in the West as cathedral window patchwork and is made from folded square units that are joined together with whipstitch to form a larger design. Small squares of fabric are inserted under the rolled hemlines of the folded edges (see pages 32–33).

The first documented evidence of this design used in a quilt or bed covering appeared at the 1933 World Trade Fair. However, its origins date back much further, with examples appearing as far back as the Joseon Dynasty in Korea. The design also appears in other East Asian cultures including the southern

Wrapping cloth for food, known as sang bo. Made from squares of sukgosa *(fine silk gauze), pieced with* garumsol *seams (whipstitch) and lined with another layer of* sukgosa. *The central tab is held in place by a bakgi mae dup (bat knot) and is used as a handle to lift the cloth.*

Detail of Jewel Pattern
*by Youngmin Lee. The
border is stitched with
settam sangchim (see
page 90).*

province of Guizhou in China. Here it is made
with an appliqué technique and often used for
baby carriers to wish the child a happy and
wealthy life. Just how the design reached
Western shores we can only guess at, but
some think it may have returned with
missionaries – hence its religious name.

Looking at the historical examples of the
jewel-pattern wrapping cloths in Dr Huh
Dong-hwa's collection (see page 28) there

is little consistency in the size of units used to
make this pattern or the overall finished size
of the piece. The size of units ranged from
8cm (3$\frac{1}{4}$in) to 3.5cm (1$\frac{3}{8}$in). Most of the
examples were finished in square designs but
there were rectangular examples as well.
Most measured around one *pok*, 35cm (14in),
but there were also bigger ones. I think we
can conclude that the maker was free to
choose whatever size unit she wanted to
make her jewel-pattern design.

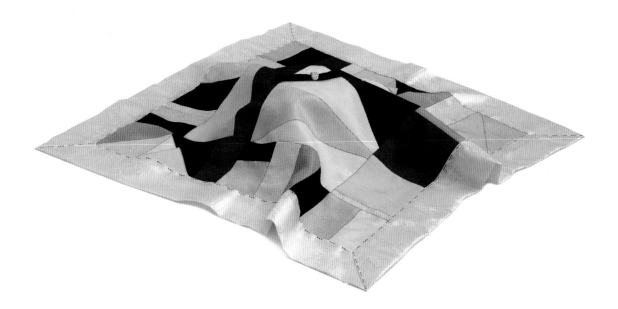

Decorative *bakgi mae dup*, or bat knots, were often added at the intersections of the seams and this served both to create a neat finish and to hold the lining fabric in place – a useful detail that was not brought back by the missionaries.

This patchwork design was usually made using very fine silk fabrics that are easily manipulated. Contrasting coloured cloths, often silk of a heavier weight, were added where the fabric was folded back to make concave sides. These were stitched down with small running or hemming stitches and formed the interlocking 'coin' or 'jewel' pattern.

While the resulting bojagi does not need to be lined, many examples do have borders formed by folding a lining fabric to the front of the work. Borders on wrapping cloths were generally created by cutting a piece of ramie fabric for the lining larger than the finished panel. This would then be folded to the front, creating a border with either straight or mitred corners. The border was held in place by decorative *settam* or *duttam sangchim*, which are blocks of two or three stitches. A handle or tab was added to the centre, secured with more bat knots. Some would be lined with oiled paper to protect them from food stains.

Since its introduction to the West the design has been reproduced and more recently developed by well-known quilters in the UK, Lynne Edwards and Jennie Raiment, who have explored rectangles and triangles as unit shapes to create many more exciting designs.

Replica of a silk covering cloth from the British Museum collection, London, c.1900. The tab handle is held in place with a bakji mae dup *(bat knot).*

Nubi means to quilt and is the name used to describe quilted wrapping cloths and all types of quilted clothing, bedding mats and small items that provided warmth or protection depending on the use.

Saeksil nubi is quilting that uses fine strips of hand-rolled hanji paper, held in narrow channels of geometric patterns, worked in back stitch with coloured threads on a plain background (see page 120).

Nubi wrapping cloth by Eun Jin Jeong. Narrow rows of hand-stitched quilting on two layers of myeongju (plain silk) with obangsaek striped fabric for the ties. This contemporary bojagi references the ancient tradition of using paper for covering food by placing a circle of oiled hanji paper at the centre.

20th-century influences

As with so many beautiful functional objects made anonymously by women throughout the ages, bojagi was not recognized as an art form until relatively recently. Collectors like the late Dr Huh Dong-hwa, Director of the Museum of Korean Embroidery, did much to save examples of bojagi at a time when it was not valued. His private collection of over 13,000 bojagi, now destined for a state museum in Seoul, began in the 1960s when he noticed that the antique furniture he was collecting was often bundled up with discarded wrapping cloths. His collection changed at that point to bojagi and he would sometimes buy a piece of furniture he didn't want just in order to obtain the wrapping cloth.

Korea was occupied by Japan from 1910 to 1945, who declared the country a part of their dominion. During that period, cultural traditions were suppressed, speaking Korean was forbidden and everyone was required to change their Korean names to Japanese ones. Shintoism became the national religion with no other religious beliefs tolerated. Cultural buildings were destroyed or used in a disrespectful way. Many other privations were experienced, and when the country was liberated in 1945, many children who had been born and grown up during this period were unable to read or speak Korean. The Korean War that followed liberation was bitterly fought, leaving the country one of the poorest in the world. Divided in 1954 into North Korea and South Korea along the

19th century postcard showing Korean women dressed in traditional hanbok *clothes. They are calendaring fabric, possibly ramie or hemp, by beating the fabric with wooden batons while it is held under tension.*

38th parallel, it took tenacious hard work and suffering to build South Korea into the wealthy and successful nation that it is today. That long march towards success took its toll on cultural traditions such as bojagi.

Until the 20th century, there was little contact between Korea and the West. Chinese and Japanese culture had been influential on Western design for hundreds of years but Korea remained outside of this oriental genre. Conversely, it is only since the second half of the 20th century that Western design has had an influence in South Korea. The result may be that cultural traditions have remained in living memory even with the long period of Japanese occupation.

Textile artists such as Chunghie Lee have brought this ancient craft to our attention with their own contemporary work in this style. Chunghie Lee's *No Name Woman* (see page 71) celebrated all those unknown women who created beautiful bojagi, often in isolated conditions. An ambassador for bojagi, she has worked tirelessly to bring these textiles to our notice through organizing exhibitions and forums.

Like most traditions, there are discrepancies and regional differences. With few records preserved and made by the women whose lives in general were not documented by history, different methods of construction have evolved.

Durumagi by Chunghie Lee. Chunghie Lee has used traditional sukgosa (fine silk gauze) and kkekki seams to celebrate form and function of an iconic Korean garment, the durumagi (long overcoat).

In a confident economic environment, South Korea has invested in preserving its cultural traditions and has a system of creating national treasures. Designated makers and artists who have been deemed as outstanding experts in their field are granted a lifetime government stipend. Assistants are trained so that their knowledge is passed on, ensuring its future. This extends to all of the arts, where textile traditions are valued equally alongside what are sometimes considered more traditional art forms.

During the Chuseok Festival (Korean Thanksgiving Day) I witnessed exquisite silk-wrapped gifts being carried by people returning to their family homes, showing that the tradition still survives, even if those wrapping cloths were of a commercial mass-produced type rather than beautifully crafted by hand.

Blue Rain (2012) by
Marianne Pemberthy,
48 x 122cm (19 x 48in).
Silk organza, acid dye,
hand-stitched with
machine-embroidery.

Metamorphosis *by
Leonie Castelino. A
three-dimensional piece
made up of three layers,
using silk organza and
Procion dye, pieced with
kkekki seams.*

Textile artists, fashion designers, quilters and embroiderers the world over can now be seen to
embrace the principles of bojagi to express their creative ideas in exciting ways. The designers
at Chanel fashion house took inspiration from *jogakbo* (bojagi made with small scraps of fabric)
for their resort collection in 2016. The revival of interest of this traditional style of stitched
textile both in the West and in Korea has ensured its survival and continued development.

PROJECT: jewel pattern

You will need two different weights of thread for this technique. A lighter weight one such as a 60 weight thread in cotton or silk for piecing the squares together, and a heavier weight such as a 40 or 30 for stitching the folded edges down.

Traditionally, lighter weight fabrics such as silk organza or fine silk were used to make this design. You could also use lightweight silk taffeta, fine cotton lawn, organdie or linen. If the fabric you want to use is soft to handle then starch it before you begin working (see page 42 for instructions on making and using rice starch).

For this example, I am going to make two finished units measuring 5cm (2in) square. Follow the imperial measurements or the metric measurements, but do not mix the two as conversions are not exact.

YOU WILL NEED

2 pieces lighter weight fabric measuring 12cm (4¹/₂in) square

1 piece contrasting coloured heavier weight fabric (or two layers of lighter weight fabric) measuring 3cm (1¹/₂in) square

Cutting mat

Fabric creaser or Hera marker

Needle

60 weight thread

30 or 40 weight thread

scissors

Iron (dry)

Pins

1 Place both large squares of fabric on the cutting mat and using your creaser mark a 7mm (¹/₄ in) seam allowance on all four edges. Fold the seam allowance to the wrong side along the creased lines.

2 Find the centre of each square by folding in half diagonally and vertically. Mark this by finger creasing the central part of these lines where they intersect.

3 Thread your needle with a single lighter weight thread and put a knot on the end. Bring your needle up from the right side through the centre point of one square and spear each corner in turn, drawing them towards the marked centre point. Make sure your needle just catches the edge of the fabric on each corner.

4 Take your needle back through the centre point and pull the thread taught. Do not cut off your thread. Finger crease the folded edges flat, making sure that all the outside corners are really sharp. Then press with a dry iron.

5 Using the needle and thread already attached, spear the four newly created corners, drawing them towards the centre. Pass the needle through to the other side. Finger crease the folded edges of the square and then press with a dry iron. Finish off with a tiny backstitch and a firm knot at the centre, using the thread already attached. Cut off the excess thread. Repeat steps 3–5 for the second square.

6 Place the two units right sides together. The right sides look like envelopes. Thread a needle with lighter weight thread and put a

knot on the end. Hide the knot in the folds of the fabric and whipstitch the edges of the units together. Your stitches need to be about 2mm (¹⁄₁₆in) apart. Your needle needs to pass through all the layers, but try to keep the stitches close to the folded edges. You do not want to form a ridge once the two units are opened out flat. Open out the units.

7 Place the contrasting square of fabric over the central square formed across the joined units. Trim this down, if necessary, so that about 3mm (¹⁄₈in) of background fabric shows all around. Pin in place.

8 Beginning in one corner, roll the biased border over onto the contrasting square. This will form a curved edge. Stitch this in place with either a hemming stitch or running stitch. Try to make the same number of stitches along each side, keeping to odd numbers. Five or seven is a good number to use: these are auspicious. Four would be considered unlucky. At each corner, draw the edges together with a double bar tack, and your piece is finished.

Opposite: Detail from Luminous #1 by Youngmin Lee (see page 22). You can see why Westerners renamed the jewel pattern 'Cathedral Windows'.

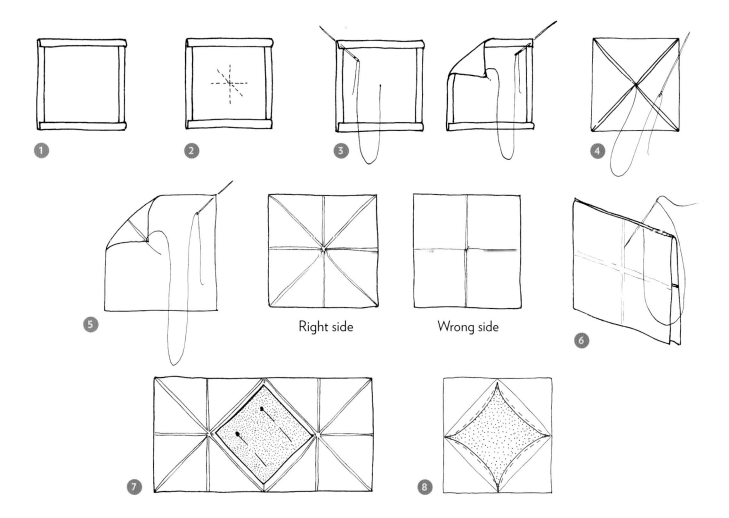

Right side   Wrong side

CHAPTER 2

FABRICS AND SEWING EQUIPMENT

Fabric

Traditionally, wrapping cloths were made from different types and weights of fine silk cloth, including brocades and organza, as well as cotton, hemp and ramie. These fabrics all have a crisp quality that makes them perfect for sewing bojagi by hand. All can be dyed using natural dyes or fibre-reactive cold-water dyes. Silk fabrics take up dye much more readily than cellulose fabrics, and bright colours are therefore easier to achieve. Hemp, ramie and cotton will generally have more muted tones compared to silk. Today, contemporary makers use all types of fabrics that are available to them including those made from plastic.

Ramie (*mosi*)

Ramie fabric was used in ancient Egypt and was known in Europe during the Middle Ages. It has been cultivated in eastern Asia since prehistoric times and was exported to Europe early in the 18th century.

It is a 'bast' fibre, meaning that, like linen, the fibres are harvested from the stalk of the plant rather than the seed head, like cotton. Ramie belongs to the nettle family and does not require large amounts of water to grow. It is a sustainable crop that can be harvested two or three times a year – more if conditions are favourable – and plants live up to 20 years. Historically every village in Korea would have grown ramie and hemp alongside their other crops.

Ramie fibre is pure white in colour, lustrous, moisture absorbent, and takes up dye reasonably well. It becomes more lustrous with wear and is stronger when wet than dry, making it a very durable fibre. It is very cool to wear in the summer. The crisp quality of the fabric makes it stand away from the body, allowing air to circulate. These same crisp qualities make it perfect for making bojagi as it is possible to crease a line to sew along.

In Korea, ramie is known as *mosi*. It is often available in narrow widths approximately one *pok*, 35cm (14 in), wide. This may be because of the narrow looms that were traditionally used to produce the cloth. The fibres have to be kept wet when they are being woven as they are otherwise inclined to become brittle and snap. Most ramie cloth is now produced in China but a few artisanal producers can still be found in Korea. Its production is one of the celebrated crafts of Korea.

Ramie (top), hemp (centre) and unbleached hemp (bottom).

Hemp
(samhae)

Hemp is said to be the oldest fabric produced in Korea. A number of historical records including the *Samguk Sagi* (*The History of the Three Kingdoms*), written in the 12th century, show that a *sambae* weaving contest was part of the annual Chuseok (Korean Thanksgiving Day) events in Gyeongju. Hemp remains have been found on Chinese pottery dating back 10,000 years, and in medieval Europe hemp was grown for domestic cloth, sails and rope because it was easier to grown than linen. Hemp plants produce a high ratio of fibre to land used, making it a very economical crop. By the 19th century, 80 per cent of the world's fabric was made of hemp.

Hemp and ramie for sale at the fabric market in Seoul, Korea.

It is a sustainable crop that does not deplete the soil and has been referred to as the world's most useful plant. It is also a 'bast' fibre and it can be dyed. Like ramie, hemp was traditionally favoured for summer clothes as it is cool to wear. It was worn by ordinary people for everyday wear and by the wealthy for mourning clothes. It can also be stiffened, making it stand away from the body, a quality that makes it perfect for taking a crease when making bojagi. Today the best hemp cloth in South Korea is produced in Andong, where its production is considered to be one of the celebrated crafts of Korea and enjoys state recognition.

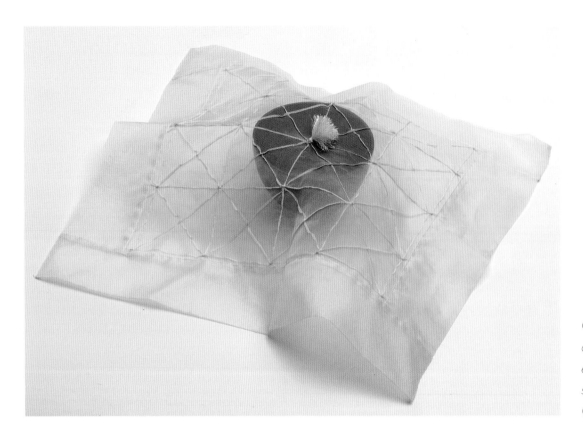

Silk

China is the oldest producer of silk fabrics and records of sericulture, or silk production, can be found
as far back as 3,000–5,000BC. The Silk Road, an ancient network of interconnected routes that linked
Beijing to the coast of the Mediterranean, was established in the 2nd century BC. Chinese silk fabrics
were thought to have reached Rome. China closely guarded the secret of sericulture until the
2nd century AD, when silk cocoons were smuggled out by a Chinese princess in her wedding clothes
to the province of Khotan, an ancient Iranian city that became famous for its silk production.

Evidence for the knowledge of silk production in Korea can be found mentioned in the 12th century
Samguk Sagi (*The History of the Three Kingdoms*) and the best silk was said to be have been
produced in what is now North Korea.

Silk fibres are produced from the cocoons created by the larvae of the silk moth (*Bombyx mori*)
and are a protein fibre. Once the fibres have been degummed they can be spun and woven into a
wide range of different weights of fabric. Silk takes up dye really well, so that bright colours can be
produced. It has the wonderful quality of feeling cool in the summer and warm in the winter because
it is a poor conductor of electricity.

TYPES OF SILKS SUITABLE FOR MAKING WRAPPING CLOTHS

Chinese organza is similar in appearance to organdie, with a smooth, uniform surface that is translucent. It is widely available in white and black as well as a large range of colours. Strong continuous filaments of silk thread are used in the warp fibres of the loom, making this a strong and springy fabric that is less likely to fray. It dyes well and is very versatile.

Korean organza (*nobang*) is available in the traditionally narrow one *pok*, 35cm (14in), width and has an opaque appearance. The slub surface is made up of uneven stripes of variable density across the width of the cloth, showing more character than the uniform surface of Chinese silk organza. Used for covering cloths for food, it has a crisp handle that keeps its shape but its relatively loose weave means that it is inclined to fray.

Plain weave silk is known as *myeongju* and is the type of silk used for making *nubi* (quilted clothing) and *saeksil nubi* (corded quilting).

Silk gauze (*sukgosa*) is a fine-weight fabric. These are plain-coloured fabrics with a self pattern including lots of auspicious symbols. They are used for making traditional summer-weight clothes (*hanbok*) and the leftover scraps would have been used to make *jogakbo* covering cloths.

Silk satin is known as *gongdan*. This is a heavier weight silk that would have been worn in the cooler seasons, often with brocaded designs of auspicious symbols. This is a high-value fabric that would have been worn by the wealthy.

Korean organza (top), Chinese organza (centre) and sukgosa (fine gauze silk) in grey, yellow and blue patterned with symbols of longevity, good luck and happiness woven into the fabric (bottom).

Alternative fabrics

Fine linen can be used in place of the ramie or hemp fabrics, and the Chinese organza that is widely available makes a great alternative to the traditional weights and qualities used in Korea. Cotton organdie has a crisp finish which is also great for making bojagi. All of these alternative fabrics will dye well.

Polyester organzas are less suitable as they are inclined to fray and slip in the hand. If your fabrics are soft to handle then it's best to starch them well before you start cutting.

COTTON (*MUMYEONG*)

Brought to Korea in the 14th century from China, it was once one of the top three commodities of the Joseon Dynasty and was exported to Japan.

Cotton organdie is a plain-weave, translucent fabric that comes in three types; semi stiffened, stiff and soft. It has a crisp finish brought about by a series of chemical finishing processes. Not all organdie fabrics are treated with a permanent starched finish so washing a small piece first will reveal whether the treatment is permanent or not.

The fabric is immersed in an acid bath to create smooth fibres followed by a further process known as mercerization where the fabric is dipped into a strong alkaline solution such as lithium hydroxide, caustic soda, or potassium hydroxide, so that the fibres in the fabric will appear more lustrous when finished. Mercerization is named after John Mercer who invented the process in 1844 although it was not widely used until the 1890s.

The characteristics of organdie make it a good substitute for harder-to-find fabrics from Korea. It takes dye well, is translucent, does not fray readily and will hold a crease, which is perfect for hand piecing.

LINEN

Linen, like ramie and hemp, is a bast fibre and is one of the oldest fibres produced in the world, believed to have been first produced by the Mesopotamians in 5000BC. The Egyptians developed a sophisticated linen industry that produced gossamer-like fabric that has never been replicated since. Good-quality linen has a smooth surface and is virtually slub-free. It is only poorer quality linen that has a rough, slubbed surface.

Linen is stronger than cotton and actually becomes more polished and smooth with wear. It is extremely long lasting (the linen cloth used to wrap Egyptian mummies is evidence of that). Like ramie, it has a crisp quality that makes it stand away from the body, so it is cool to wear and also suitable for wrapping cloths. It is very absorbent so will take up dye well, plus it is easy to make a crease line in linen.

The Blues #1 (2016) by Marielle Huijsman, 75 x 150cm (29$\frac{1}{2}$ x 59in). Traditional western patchwork and quilting techniques are blended with traditional bojagi techniques of piecing. The design appears to be dissolving, revealing an underlying grid.

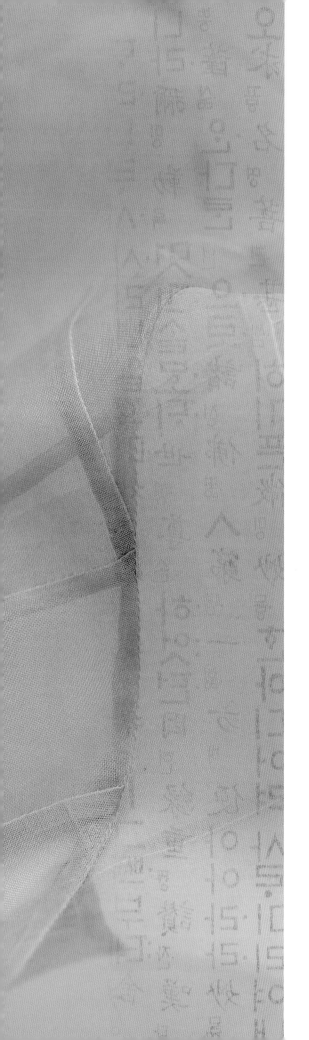

Starch

Starching makes loose-woven fabrics easier to handle, making the seams less likely to fray before they have been sewn together.

To improve the crisp handle of fabrics for making traditional wrapping cloths you can use a commercial spray starch.

Traditionally rice starch was used to stiffen fabrics in Korea. This is still widely used in some Eastern countries and it is now becoming popular again among quilters who prefer to make their own starch. I use the following recipe:

YOU WILL NEED

1 tablespoon rice flour

120ml (4fl oz) water

1 Whisk the two ingredients together to form a lump-free solution.

2 Add 500ml (17fl oz) water to a saucepan and bring this to the boil.

3 Add the rice solution and whisk continuously over a high heat until the solution looks opaque.

4 Allow it to cool. Keep in the fridge to prevent it going mouldy.

TO USE

Soak your fabric in water for 5–10 minutes in a large bowl or bucket to ensure that it is thoroughly wet through. You need to make sure that your fabric and starch solution can be moved around in the water freely. Packing your bucket or bowl with too much fabric will give uneven results.

• Wring out the excess water and discard.

• Refill your bucket or bowl with approximately 4 litres (7 pints) of cold water.

• At this point, you can add all of your solution to the bucket or for a less stiffened finish you could reduce the amount by half.

TO DRY

Spread your fabric out to dry flat if you can in the sunshine on a clean surface. I spread mine out on the lawn or hang on the washing line. DO NOT put your starched fabrics in the tumble dryer – they could scorch and silk fabrics especially may lose their lustre.

Don't leave your fabrics drying in the sun for too long. Once they are dry, bring them in to avoid causing the colours to fade.

TO IRON

Iron your fabric on a medium to hot setting. Too hot and the starch will scorch and leave brown marks on the iron and possibly your fabric too.

Sewing equipment

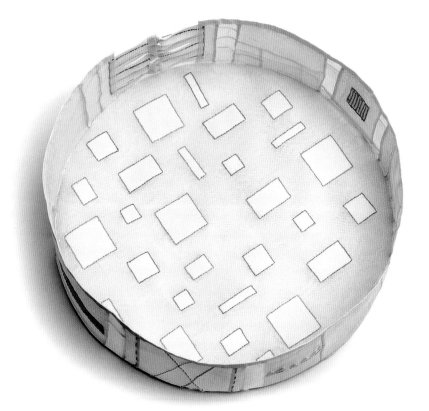

A *banjitgori* or sewing box was where a woman kept her seven sewing friends: needle, thread, a thimble, a ruler, a pair of scissors, a small iron called an *indoo* and a large iron with a bowl to carry charcoal called a *darimi*. These would have been kept in either a basket or a wooden or papier-mâché box and were an essential part of every home.

For hand piecing, modern sewers add a rotary cutter and mat, creaser and pins to that list as well.

Left: Banjitgori *made from Korean silk organza, hanji paper and silk thread.*

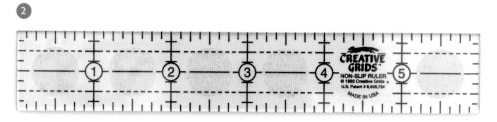

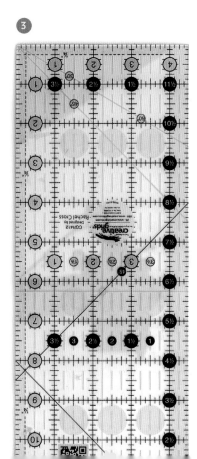

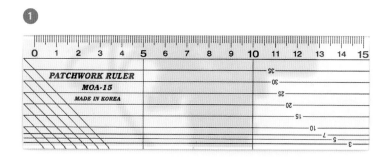

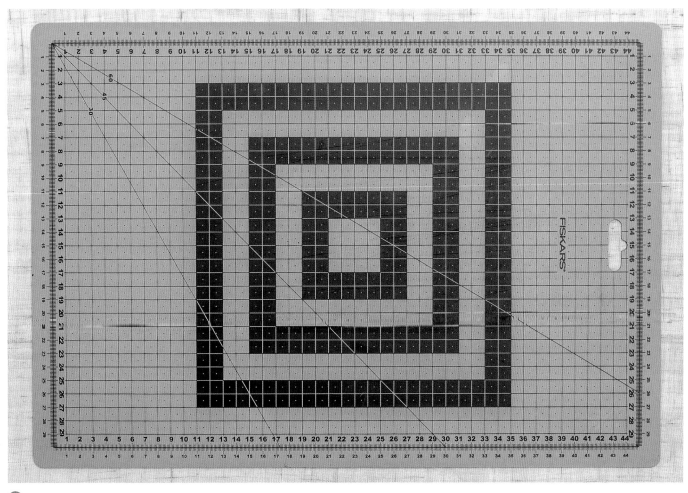

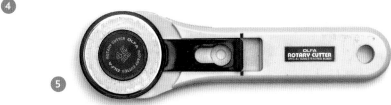

Korean metric acrylic ruler (1); 1 x 6in imperial acrylic ruler (2); 41/2 x 12in imperial acrylic ruler (3); rotary cutting mat (4); 45mm rotary cutter (5); 0.5mm needles (6).

NEEDLES

The size of needle for making traditional hand-pieced bojagi depends on the thickness of fabric that you are working with. When piecing the finest of silks you need to work with a fine needle. I like to use a #9 Milliners Straw (42.4mm x 0.56mm diameter) as this glides though the fabric easily and helps making those tiny overcast stitches more achievable. Thicker needles are needed for heavier weight fabrics and threads. I have found using size 9 appliqué needles are also a good alternative. The thicker the thread you choose to use the bigger the needle you will need.

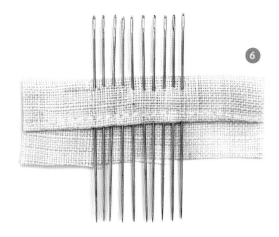

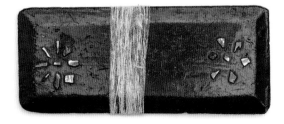

THREAD

Silk threads were used to join silk fabrics together. Different weights of silk thread were used for decorative stitching and for embroidery. Cotton thread was used to join the ramie, cotton and hemp fabrics.

Ramie and hemp fabrics can be difficult to hand sew with a normal 50 weight thread as the thread wears quickly and is inclined to break. 40 or 30 weight cotton hand quilting threads are more suitable, especially those with a wax coating as this protects the thread as it passes through the fabric. Alternatively, you could use a block of dressmakers' wax to coat a thread yourself by passing it through the wax several times. Quilting threads with a mixed fibre, polyester and cotton are also stronger and work well.

Other threads that can be used include stranded embroidery threads. These have a sheen and can be used singly or doubled depending on how bold you want to make the stitches. Many manufacturers now produce gorgeous ranges of coloured threads which are available in a rainbow of colours. When creating your work, take time to select a thread that will enhance the overall finish, deciding whether you want it to match or create a contrasting effect.

Fine silk thread and 40 weight cotton quilting thread for piecing silk or ramie (1); Threads for piecing silk fabrics (2); Mulberry silks for fine piecing and decorative stitching (3); Antique Korean thread winder (4); Embroidered thimbles (5); Silk pins (6); Hera marker or creaser (7).

THIMBLE (*GOLMU*)

There is a Korean saying that 100 thimbles in a box will bring longevity. A Korean bride during the Joseon Dynasty would embroider her thimbles with auspicious symbols, giving them to the women of the groom's family as a way of conveying her respect by wishing them long and happy lives.

They were made from two layers of fabric that were padded with layers of hanji paper or cotton fabric to make them stiff and impenetrable. These were then covered with brightly coloured and embroidered silk before being joined together with a dense overlapping cross stitch.

PINS

It is worth seeking out good-quality pins. There are many brands of silk pins available but not all of them are the same thickness. Look for brands that have 0.4mm diameter and that have a good sharp point. Using thicker pins will move the fabric around and decrease your chances of accuracy. Thicker pins will leave holes in the fabric. IBC Silk pins or Clover silk pins are both fine and strong.

CREASERS

Also known as Hera markers or bone folders, in bojagi making they are used together with a ruler to mark a seam allowance along which the fabric is folded before stitching. Hera markers are made of a solid plastic with a sharpened edge that when pressed firmly onto fabric along a ruler will leave a faint line where the fibres have been polished. This eliminates any need to draw a seam allowance with a pencil or marking pen. It works particularly well on stiffened fabrics. The fabric folds easily along the creased line. They are also used for marking out the lines of *khojipgi*, the pinching technique.

At one time these markers were made from a leg bone of a cow or deer, but now are much more likely to be plastic, although bamboo and wooden creasers are also available.

MAKING A STARTING KNOT IN YOUR THREAD

All the hand work that I learnt in Korea always began with a knot made this way. Starting with a backstitch, as I had been trained to do since learning to sew as a child, has been usurped by this idea. It is a strong and neat way to start and finish lines of hand sewing. It makes more sense to complete a row of whipstitch with a finishing knot than with a backstitch. Quilters will recognise this knot as a way to start and finish lines of hand quilting.

1 Put the tail of your thread along the length of the needle and hold it firmly between your thumb and finger.

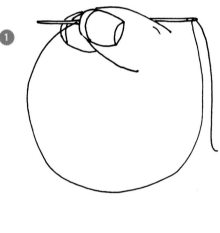

2 Wind this thread around the needle point three times, close to the position of your thumb and finger.

3 Trap these loops under your thumb and finger (you might find it easier to change hands at this point). Pull the needle through with your right hand (left-handers with your left hand).

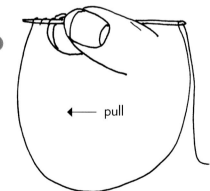

4 Pull the needle away from the thumb and finger all the while pinching firmly. You should feel a small knot forming at you pull the thread through. Trim the tail of the thread near to the knot.

FINISHING KNOT

1 To finish a seam, place the needle at right angles to the seam edge and close to where the last stitch was made.

2 Wind the thread around the needle three times, close to the point.

3 Trap the loops under your thumb and finger and pinch together. Pull the needle until all the thread has passed through the wound loops of thread. Use your fingernail to stop the loops escaping and pull the last bit firmly to make a neat, tight knot. Trim the thread close to the knot.

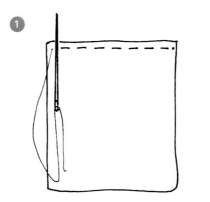

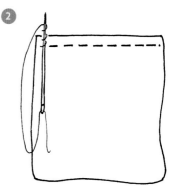

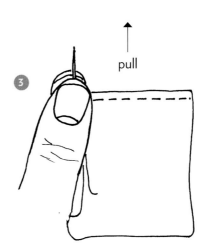

pull

CHAPTER 3

COLOUR,
DESIGN AND
SYMBOLISM

Aesthetics

Eastern aesthetic ideas have historically been influenced by philosophical and religious beliefs. While China has exerted a strong influence on Korean culture, much of its influence has been modified by a Korean aesthetic sensibility that has its origins in Korean history and the natural environment. The harmonizing of contrasting objects is important. This is based on the Taoist belief that beauty and ugliness are only human perceptions.

Suwon (Hwaseong) Fortress, Suwon, Korea. You can see the traditional use of the ogansaek colours in the decorative paintwork. Bakgi good luck symbols are incorporated in the roof tiles.

Western aesthetic design is traditionally based on the classical principles that great art cannot exist without proportion and number. Symmetry, perspective, scale, proportion and representative endeavours were considered the Holy Grail of great art. Beauty achieved by perfect mathematical proportions based on Pythagorean principles. These ideals have, of course, been challenged since the mid-19th century by the Modernist movement, which has sought to overthrow such restrictions.

It is impossible to ignore aesthetic ideas when looking at Korean wrapping cloths. The maker would have chosen colours and symbols according to ideals passed down through the centuries.

Yin and yang

It was the belief that the conscious composition of certain colours would bring good luck and prevent evil. The yin and yang colours of blue, yellow and red with white and black were thought to repel evil spirits and welcome happiness. Blue and red represent balance and harmony, positive and negative, masculine and feminine, hot and cold. This idea is based in Taoism, a Chinese philosophy from the 3rd century BC. The basic premise is to encourage you to live your life in a balanced way, in harmony with the world around you. The dark swirl of the symbol represents the yin and the light swirl the yang. Each side has a dot of colour from the other, because everything contains the seed of its opposite. Yin and yang describe how seemingly opposite or contrary forces may actually be complementary, interconnected and interdependent.

A yin-yang symbol on the entrance doors to the Dosan Seowon Confucian academy.

Yin and yang can be contrasting but complementary ideas that work together to create a unified whole. This belief can be seen through the use of sun and moon, male and female, in the painted *irworobongdo* screens displayed behind the King in the throne hall in the royal palace. The name *irworobongdo* literally means 'painting of the sun, moon and the five peaks'. A highly stylized landscape painting of a sun and a full moon symbolize the King's place in the universe in the form of the sun and the Queen is represented by the moon. The five peaks represent the five celebrated mountains that circle the Korean peninsula.

The symbolic use of colour is evident in traditional clothing, wrapping cloths and embroidery. The five colours (blue, red, yellow, white and black), representing the four points of the compass plus the centre, were often used in making bojagi. Wedding bojagi would often make use of these colours along with a traditional knot signifying the joining of the two families as well as other symbols. A wedding wrapping cloth that I viewed in Bukchon in Seoul was made from two layers of brocaded silk satin. An outer layer of red and a blue lining which, when opened, would have revealed the yellow golden symbols of good fortune and longevity imprinted in gold leaf on the fabric.

Obangsaek:
The five cardinal colours of Korea

Obangsaek are the traditional five cardinal colours of Korea. Blue, red, yellow, white and black. These five colours correspond to the four points or directions of the compass with yellow at the centre. These colours correspond to the five elements of the weather (cold, warmth, wind, dryness and humidity), the five elements of the universe (wood, fire, water, metal and earth); the five seasonal differences (spring, summer, autumn, winter and *toyong*, the 18 transitional days preceding each season) and the five blessings (longevity, wealth, success, health and luck).

Historically, strict sumptuary laws restricted the choices of clothing that different classes of people could wear. This extended to fabric and colour. The wealthy were allowed to wear the best brightly coloured silks in the yin-yang colours of blue and red, while the poor had to make do with lower-quality fabrics in subdued colours. Ordinary citizens were forbidden from wearing bright colours, especially yellow, a colour reserved for kings and emperors – to do so was to risk execution.

We can see these five colours in the South Korean flag and they remain significant in Korea today. Traditional costume is worn for weddings, Chuseok (a national holiday that corresponds to the full moon day of the eighth lunar month), special birthdays and New Year's Day.

Colour	Direction	Element	Season	Symbolic creature
Blue (Yin)	East	Wood	Spring	Blue dragon
White	West	Metal	Autumn	White tiger
Yellow	Centre	Earth	*Toyong*	Yellow dragon
Red (Yang)	South	Fire	Summer	Phoenix
Black	North	Water	Winter	Black tortoise

Obangsaek – *the five cardinal colours of Korea – blue, red, yellow, white and black.*

Ogansaek bracelet showing the five cardinal colours plus additional secondary colours. Popularly made by children by threading garakji knots tied from colourful cords onto an elastic one.

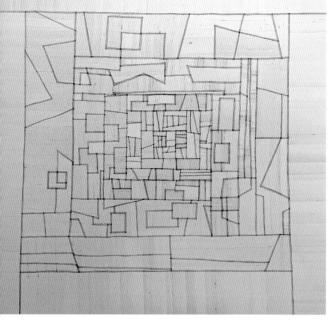

WHITE

White has strong historical significance for Korea. In the 3rd century AD the Chinese called the Koreans 'the white clad people', which refers to the universal wearing of undyed ramie fabric. Royal mandates issued during the Silla period (57BC–935AD) forbade the wearing of imperial colours, symbols or decorations including embroidery. The restrictions were applied to the nobility as well as the ordinary people and may be one of the reasons why white ramie clothes persisted even when restrictions were later relaxed.

White remains a popular choice in Korea – and was used in the Pyeong Chang 2018 Olympic Winter Games. The Korean mascot was a white tiger, demonstrating the continued belief and significance of this colour.

White is said to represent the direction of the west, the metal element and the autumn season. The white tiger is said to protect the west and to control the winds.

BLACK

Black represents the direction of the north, the element of water and the season of winter. The guardian of this direction is the black tortoise, which symbolizes wisdom, long life, darkness and calm. The black tortoise is also said to have strong yin energy and to have the power to control ghosts, which are beings of lesser yin energy.

BLUE

Blue represents the direction of east, the element of wood, and the season of spring whose guardian is the blue dragon. Blue brings to mind spring and new beginnings or rain and clouds. Koreans used to view blue and green as variations of the same colour. Green now has its own name in the Korean language.

RED

Red represents the south, the element of fire and the season of summer. The guardian of the south is the phoenix. With its strong yang energy, the phoenix can control the lives of living things and beat back death and evil spirits, the opposite of the tortoise of the north. Red also represents life, passion and creation.

YELLOW

Yellow is the centre, representing the earth and sun. It encompasses all four seasons. It is the most important colour as it symbolizes the brightest light in the world. It is also a perfect balance of yin and yang energy. Some say its guardian animal is a yellow dragon. It was the colour only to be worn by kings and members of the court. In the Silla period (57BC–935AD) royal mandates meant that anyone else seen wearing this colour would face punishment that might even mean death.

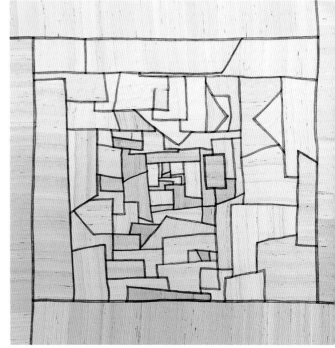

OGANSAEK

This is another set of five colours used in traditional Korean design. Two *obangsaek* colours are mixed to make *ogansaek* colours: green (yellow + blue), light blue (blue + white), pink (red + white), sulphur yellow (yellow + black) and violet (red + blue). Though *obangsaek* is more representative than *ogansaek* as Korea's traditional colours, they are used harmoniously in traditional designs.

Obangsaek *by Yoko Kubota. One layer of pieced Korean silk using* ssamsol *(fell seams), each representing one of the five cardinal colours.*

The ten symbols of longevity

Many fabrics used to make bojagi have symbols woven into their design, while other are painted or embroidered with auspicious motifs.

There are ten longevity symbols in Korea: sun, bamboo, cloud, crane, deer, mountain, mushroom, pine tree, turtle and waves. You will find these symbols used in roof tiles, woven into fabric and used in embroidery designs. They are Taoist symbols that imply good luck and blessings for a long life.

The symbols can also be seen printed onto textiles in the unique process of *keum-boo*, gold imprinted onto fabric. Carved wooden blocks are used to print a glue made from fish onto the fabric, and 24 carat gold foil is applied over the top. Contemporary makers could substitute modern foiling techniques to hint at this ancient tradition.

Many of these symbols have Animistic, Shamanistic, Taoist and Confucian roots that have variously played an important part in the spiritual and religious history of Korea. Humans were seen as part of nature, not separate from it, and the goal was to live in harmony with all aspects of the natural world.

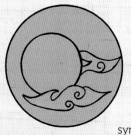

SUN

Probably the most important of the ten symbols, the sun is identified with longevity because it rises in the sky each day, without fail. The sun and moon represent the complementary yet opposing forces yin and yang, which animate the cosmos in East Asian philosophy. The sun is pure yang, the male principle of the universe that is light, active and generates life.

PINE TREE

The pine tree is one of the most common symbols of longevity in East Asia. Because it remains green even in the harshest winters, it stands for resilience, endurance, and strength against adversity. Its gnarled bark was thought to resemble an old man's skin. The pine tree, bamboo and plum tree are sometimes referred to as the Three Friends of Winter, perhaps because they are evergreens.

CRANE

It was believed that cranes could live for a 1,000 years, after which their feathers turned black. In fact some species do live as long as eighty years. Cranes mate for life, and therefore symbolize harmony, a wish for a long marriage, and respect for one's parents and ancestors.

WAVES

Wave designs symbolize the seas and waters of the earth and different patterns describe the waters as calm or rough. These designs are most commonly seen as stylized semicircles superimposed on one another. A universal symbol of life, fruitfulness, and abundance, water is linked to longevity across time and is one of the five eternal elements – together with earth, fire, metal and wood – that make up the cosmos.

CLOUD

Clouds are symbolic of heaven and long life and appear in endless variations in fabric design and embroidery. They were often used as filler patterns in embroidered designs. Clouds hanging around mountaintops that were thought to be the home of the immortals are said to represent the uniting of yin and yang, soft and hard, changeability and permanence, and to be eternal.

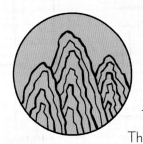

MOUNTAIN

Mountains are one of the most important Taoist symbols as they signify permanence. There are five peaks depicted on the *irworobongdo* screen in the King's throne room, representing the five peaks that circle the Korean peninsula: Geumgangsan (Kumgang) in the east, Myohyangsan in the west, Jirisan in the south, Baekdusan in the north and Samgaksan in the centre. Geumgangsan was believed to be home to the immortals, heavenly maidens, magical deer and the mushrooms of immortality. Today, there are still many temples and shrines there. In Korea and China, important state rituals were conducted in the mountains. And the mountains is where the 'mushrooms of immortality', or *lingzhi*, are said to grow. The breathing of mountains is believed to activate the universe.

DEER

The deer and antler symbols are ancient hunting totems. The deer was believed to have a long life because it ate the sacred mushrooms of immortality found in the woods and forest of the mountains. White Deer Lake on Jeju Island in Korea was said to be the place where immortals came 'to bathe and drink the milk of the white deer'.

MUSHROOM

The sacred, cloud-shaped *lingzhi* mushroom is said to grant immortality to those who eat it. This mushroom springs from the roots of trees that grow in the mountain regions. According to legend, it can be found only by a deer, a crane or a phoenix.

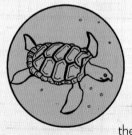

TURTLE

Turtles are noted for their long lifespan. In addition, with their dome-shaped upper shell, flat lower shell, and legs in the four corners of their bodies, they were early emblems of the universe and the cardinal directions. Often depicted with streams of breath emanating from their mouths, turtles were believed to be messengers of good news in water, their counterpart being the tiger.

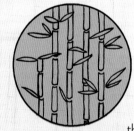

BAMBOO

Bamboo is one of the most versatile and abundant materials in East Asia, eaten by both humans and animals and used to make everything from houses to paper. It remains green throughout the four seasons and therefore symbolizes long life. Because it bends rather than breaks, bamboo also represents resilience, and its simple shape, humility. According to Confucian ideology, bamboo possesses the qualities of a great scholar: humility, uprightness, flexibility of mind and grace.

OTHER GOOD LUCK SYMBOLS

BATS

The addition of an image of a bat symbolizes wishes for good luck, happiness, health, prosperity, and joy.

FLOWERS

Lotus, plum blossom, peony and chrysanthemum are all popular symbols of good luck.

Important numbers

Four is considered an unlucky number as its symbol in Chinese is the same as for death. Many hotels avoid having a fourth floor, preferring to miss it out altogether or to label it with the letter 'F'. Five and most odd numbers are considered auspicious. When shopping in markets in Seoul I found traders would prefer me to buy five rather than four items and even threw in the fifth item to avoid invoking any bad luck. When five bat symbols are used together they represent the five fortunes of longevity, happiness, health, wealth and a natural death. The number three is a symbolic number representing the earth and the sky with man at the centre linking/joining the two realms together. Five represents the five directions (see page 54).

The central roundel contains longevity symbols surrounded by flowers and bats. Embroidery by Heehwa Jo.

Wedding-duck wrapping cloth

A *gireogibo* was a wrapping cloth made to wrap a wedding duck or goose. Mandarin ducks were chosen because it was believed that, unlike other types of ducks, they mate for life, and that if one of the pair dies, the other will mourn. It was also observed by Korean farmers that geese also mated for life so the different versions of this tale vary between goose and duck. Birds symbolize various different things in the Korean psyche; Mandarin ducks represent peace, fidelity and plentiful offspring.

Wrapping cloth in red and blue. The yin and yang colours signify balance and harmony. This detail shows groups of decorative settam sangchim *stitches.*

One story has it that a man who wished to marry would purchase pairs of live ducks or geese to give as a gift to the family of the prospective bride. Perhaps that tradition gave way to using wooden ducks in place of live animals.

Another version told to me was that the groom was supposed to carve a duck from a branch or young tree that he had felled himself. The time it took was meant to provide the young man with the opportunity for some quiet contemplation to think over this important decision.

The wrapping cloth is used to wrap two traditional wooden wedding ducks.

Others say that the couple would select a man to carve their wedding ducks who was honourable, and a good friend. Additionally, that this the man should have 'five fortunes' so that they would be imparted to the ducks and be transferred to the couple who received them. The five fortunes of the carver were that he should be: wealthy, in good health, have a good wife, not be divorced (nor should he have relatives who had been divorced), and he should have many sons. Each duck or goose was carved in two pieces, the head and neck piece fitted into the body piece and could swivel. In married life if the beaks of the ducks were turned towards each other the couple were getting along, but if they were turned away from each other the couple were not on speaking terms.

The duck or goose was presented to the bride's family the day before the wedding, wrapped in a *gireogibo* as a token of lifelong loyalty. This wrapping cloth would have been as elaborate as the groom's mother could make it, often embroidered and embellished with pine-nut decoration and *gireogi* knots.

Later in the wedding ceremony, another duck would be wrapped together with the first one, symbolizing their unity. The head and tail were usually left uncovered by the cloth. As with any tradition, each region or family would have its own interpretation.

Letters between the bride and the groom's family were traditionally exchanged ahead of the wedding. These would also have been carefully presented in bojagi.

CHAPTER 4

SEAMS AND EMBELLISHMENTS

Seams

Different types of seam were used in combination with different types and weights of fabric to make traditional bojagi. They were all worked by hand, employing stitches that are familiar to us such as running stitch, backstitch and overcasting or whipstitch.

The type of seam selected was dictated by the characteristics of the cloth and the use of the item. Fabrics that have a looser weave such as hemp and ramie are inclined to fray more easily. A seam that encloses all the raw edges, such as a *tongsol* (French seam) or *ssamsol* (fell seam) is a good solution. If a cloth was to be unlined a seam that looks as neat on the back as the front is ideal. These seams are strong and hardwearing – they are used in denim cloth garments such as jeans, which have their origins in workwear. Wrapping cloths made to carry large bundles of washing or goods are made using these seams. Conversely you will also see them used for single-layered window coverings where strength was not really required but rather a neat finish for both back and front. Seam lines are marked with a creaser and ruler. Each of the fabric pieces joined together is first folded along the creased line before stitching.

Many contemporary makers choose to piece their fabrics on the sewing machine. Some use a French seam instead. The transparent qualities of the fabrics used suggest many possibilities for designing by building up layers, using regular and irregular grids.

Detail from Greyline #1 *(see pages 106–107), showing the* tongsol *(French seams) and layers held together with* bakgi mae dup *(bat knots).*

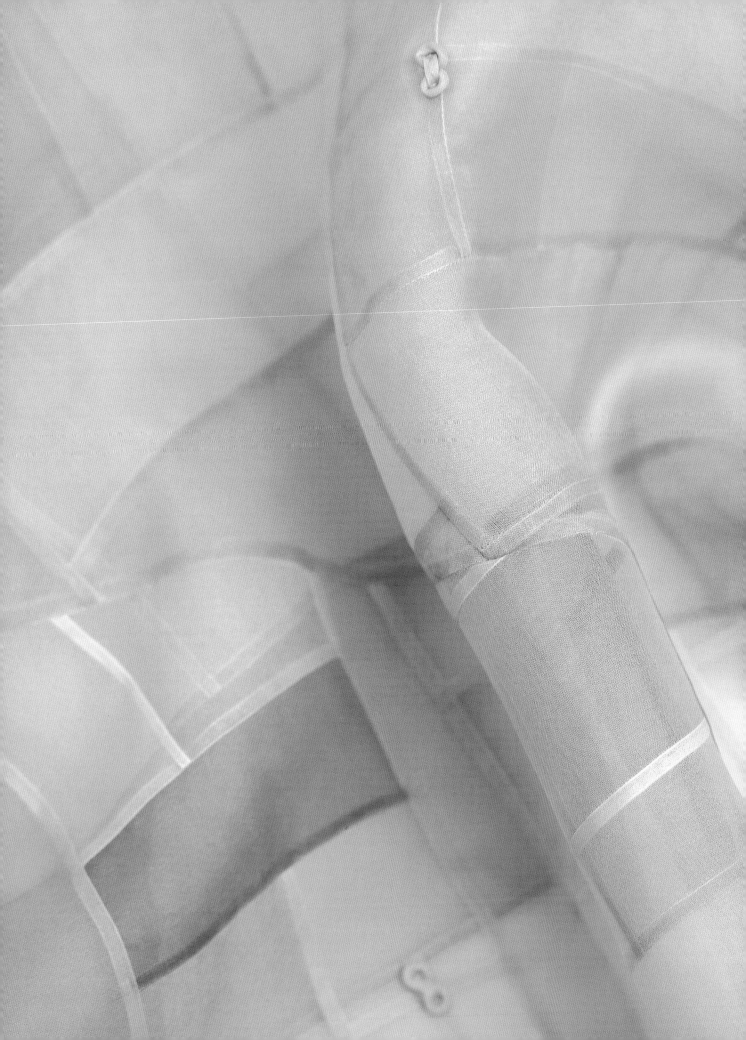

"You are beautiful Korean"

My last day in Korea, I walked around Seoul.
I had been tasked with the mission to locate a
pair of purple jelly shoes that Kat had wanted
but couldn't find in time for her flight. I woke
early before the heat would begin sticking to
me and slipped out of the apartment.

*Ryeon's Journey (2013)
by Eun Kyung Suh,
40 x 152 x 39cm
(16 x 60 x 15¹/₂in). Made
from silk organza using
French seams and photo
transfer. Using journal
entries from American
writer Ryeon Corsi's life,
this work examines the
Korean adoptees'
ambivalent feelings of
acceptance and rejection
in both societies.*

Garumsol is a seam joined using a *gamchimjil* or whipstitch, where the seam allowance is opened flat. This is used where a wrapping cloth is lined and the raw edges are hidden inside. The whipstitches were often worked in a contrasting thread from the right side. The same colour would be used throughout. The tiny stitches add another dimension to the design that is often only visible when viewed close up.

Tongsol is best described as a hand-worked French seam using *homjil*, running stitch, and it encloses all the raw edges. The difference is that the folded seam edge on the wrong side of the fabric was often sewn in place with another row of running stitch so that it has a flat finish. It is used on unlined pieces of work.

Top: Detail from The Queen *by Yoojin Kim showing* garumsol *seam. See page 100–101 for the full piece.*

Left: Ssamsol (fell seam).

Right: Chunghie Lee's No Name Woman *is a beautiful example of* kkekki *seams.*

Ssamsol is a flat fell seam stitched either with *homjil* (running stitch) or *gamchimjil* (whipstitch). This seam is used most often with bojagi made from single layers of hemp or ramie fabric. It is strong and flexible, and all the raw edges are enclosed. When completed it looks like a running fell seam popularly used in making classic denim jeans. When translucent fabrics are joined with this type of seam and are held up to the light, the pieces can look similar to stained glass. A contrasting thread was sometimes used.

Kkekki seams were made by folding and stitching the seam three times, which makes a very strong and narrow seam enclosing all the raw edges. This is most often used on lightweight fabrics such as silk organza or other very lightweight silk fabrics. Worked on heavier weight fabrics it quickly becomes too bulky. It was used for making clothing and unlined bojagi wrapping cloths.

TONGSOL (FRENCH SEAM)

An alternative to the hand-worked *tongsol* is a machine-sewn French seam. While not a traditional seam used for making wrapping cloths, it makes a good alternative to more time-consuming hand-sewn seams. This seam is borrowed from a dressmaking tradition but by making the seam allowances smaller it makes a very neat fine seam that works well with lightweight fabrics and organza. All the raw edges of the fabric are enclosed and when held up to the light it can appear like a grid or the lines of lead in stained glass.

I try to work with 3mm (1/8in) finished seam allowance. If you find this is too small then choose to start with a 12mm (1/2in) seam allowance and trim this down to 6mm (1/4in).

Banjitgori *(sewing box)*
panel pieced with tongsol
(French seams).

1 Begin by placing your fabrics *wrong* sides together. If you are stitching a long length you will want to pin the fabrics together to stop them shifting as you sew.

2 Stitch a 6mm (¹/₄in) seam using a fairly short stitch length. If your sewing machine's default straight stitch length is 2.6, reduce this to 2.

3 Trim the seam allowance to 3mm (¹/₈in).

4 Press the seam allowance to one side with the right side of the fabric facing you. Do not open the seam. Fold the fabric along the stitched line, enclosing all the raw edges. Give this a gentle press and make sure the seam line is exactly on the folded edge. Pin and stitch another 3mm (¹/₈in) seam. You may have to make this second line slightly bigger than 3mm (¹/₈in) to accommodate the bulk of the fabric. I judge this by eye. Press your seam allowance to one side when you have finished.

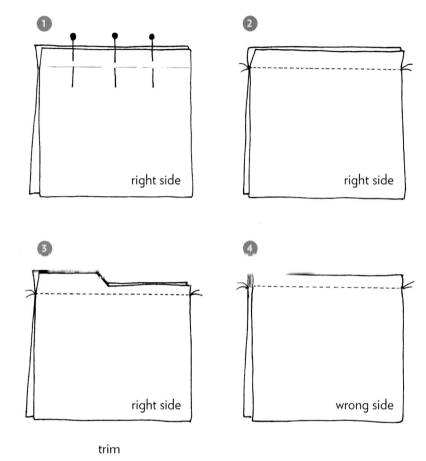

right side

right side

right side

wrong side

trim

TIP

Try moving your needle position to the right so that more of your fabric is positioned under the presser foot.

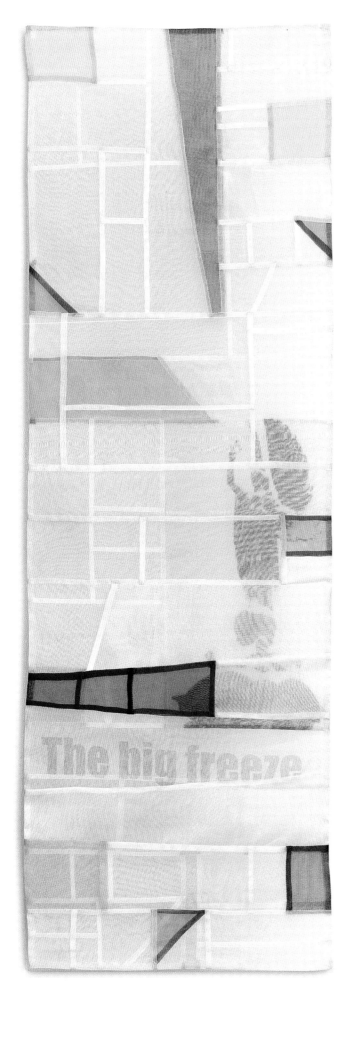

Snow (2013), 90 x 25cm (35¹/₂ x 10in). Two layers of hand-dye and photo transfer on silk organza, pieced with French seams.

GARUMSOL

This is a flat seam made by joining two pieces of fabric with whipstitch for lined wrapping cloths.

1 Lay your fabric on a cutting mat and use a ruler and creaser to mark a 6mm (¹/₄in) seam allowance on one side of each piece of fabric to be joined. Fold the seam allowance to the wrong side of the fabric.

2 Pin the two pieces of fabric wrong sides together. At this point it is up to you whether you want to use a contrasting or matching thread. Use a single thread and put a knot on the end (see page 48).

3 Begin by hiding the knot between the folds of fabric and whipstitch the edges together. Only take a small amount of fabric as you pass the needle through the folded edges of the seam. A fine needle will glide through the fabric more easily than a larger one. Sew from right to left. When you reach the end of the seam, fasten off with a knot and press the seam flat.

Banjitgori (sewing box). Jogakbo pieced panel of silk organza and silk thread showing garumsol seams stitched in yellow thread.

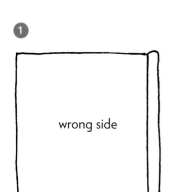

wrong side

wrong side

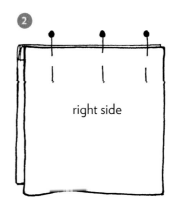

right side

TIP

Keep your needle at the same angle as you work along the seam. This will help to keep your stitches looking uniform. I keep my needle at right angles to the seam and try to space each stitch evenly.

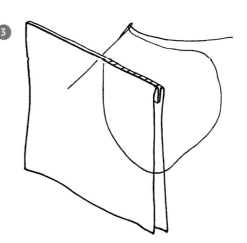

KKEKKI

Traditionally stitched by hand with running stitch, this seam can easily be made using a sewing machine. You will need to use a very short stitch length. Using a lightweight thread will also help to reduce the bulk of the seam. A 60 weight thread would be a good choice.

Once stitched, these narrow seams are extremely strong and they were used for single layers, often for clothing. All the raw edges are enclosed. They can add a dense line that contrasts beautifully with the translucency of finer fabrics.

Finished Kkekki seam.

1   Thread your needle with a single thread and
    knot the tail end. Place your fabric pieces
    right sides together and sew a row of running
    stitches along the length of the seam.

 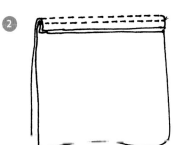

2   Fold the seam along the stitched line and
    press both seam allowances to one side. Sew
    a second row of running stitch close to the
    folded edge.

3   Trim the seam allowance close to the second
    row of running stitches.

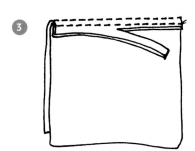 

4   Fold the seam for a second time, covering the
    raw edges. Sew a third row of running stitch
    as close to the folded edge of the seam
    allowance as you can. Press the seam to one
    side. You can choose whether you want to see
    one row of stitching or two rows. You can play
    with using different coloured threads and
    whether you make the seams on the wrong
    or right side of the work.

SSAMSOL (FLAT FELL SEAM)

This is a flat fell seam joined with whipstitch for unlined wrapping cloths.

1 Begin by marking the seam allowances using a ruler and creaser: mark a 6mm (¼in) crease line on the first piece of fabric. Fold the fabric along this line to the wrong side. On the second piece of fabric mark a 6mm (¼in) and 12mm (½in) crease line. Fold along the 12mm (½in) crease line.

2 Place wrong sides together and pin.

3 Thread your needle with a single thread and make a knot on the tail end (see page 48). Hide your knot in the fabric folds. Whipstitch the edges together and finish with a knot. Your stitches are on the right side of the fabric.

4 Open the seam and press both of the seam allowances to one side with the shorter one on top of the longer one.

5 Fold the longer seam allowance over the shorter one to cover the raw edge.

6 Fold this edge down again, enclosing all the raw edges. Mark a crease line next to this folded edge. Fold the fabric away from you along the crease line.

7 Whipstitch this edge. You are now stitching on the wrong side of the fabrics.

8 Press the seam flat.

TIP

If you are using a plain fabric without any discernible right and wrong side, make a thread tack on the side you choose as your right side on each of the pieces.

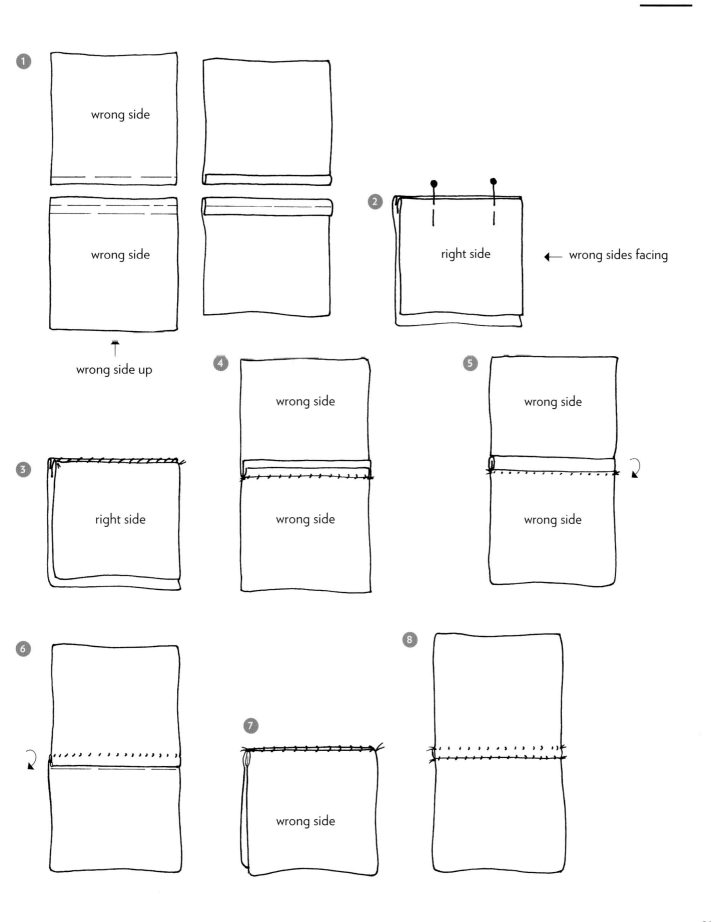

wrong side

wrong side

wrong side up

right side

wrong sides facing

right side

wrong side

wrong side

wrong side

wrong side

wrong side

Embellishments

Duttam sangchim and **settam sangchim** are decorative stitches. Arranged in groups of two (*duttam*) or three (*settam*), *sangchim* stitches are often seen around the edges of bojagi. They were mostly sewn in a contrasting thread, and were both functional and decorative. They often appear along the edges of borders where the raw edge has been turned under onto a pieced panel. They are used to hold that edge in place without any further stitching applied either before or afterwards. You often see them used to hold tie handles in place.

I have been shown how to sew these decorative straight stitches in different ways by different teachers, and from my observation of historical examples the methods of the past also seem to vary. It is true to say that the finer the quality of the fabrics and stitching then the smaller these decorative stitches are worked. Some are spaced with gaps equal to the previous group of stitches, but not always. Some have loops of thread visible on the back of the work and, more unusually, others hide the loop between the layers. All the teachers did agree, however, that these stitches are a symbol of good luck.

Bakgi mae dup or bat figure decorations are intriguing knot-like objects made from small scraps of fabric and can be often be seen on *jogakbo* patchwork bojagi. They appear at the intersection of seams, at the corners or in the centre holding a tab or handle in place. They can be used to join two layers together but have more significance than this functional purpose. It is hard to believe that portraying flying bats in embroidered designs or woven into fabric could be considered a symbol of luck until you understand that it is a play on words. The Chinese character for happiness is *bok* and is the same name as 'bat' in Korean. Both have the same sound. The bat figure therefore becomes the means for translating an auditory symbol (a word) into a visual one (a design) and the bat design becomes the symbol of happiness.

The two rounded sides of this bat symbol represent the wings of the bat. The more bats that you add to your wrapping cloth the more good luck and happiness you are bestowing on the cloth.

Left and right: Details from The Queen *by Yoojin Kim showing* setlam sangchim *stitching along the outside edge. See pages 100–101 for the complete piece.*

Jat ssi means pine nuts and these decorative points, not unlike prairie points, are traditionally added to one corner of a wedding bojagi to bring good luck. When the piece is folded, the knots are visible at the edge. Made by folding a square of fabric multiple times, they were inserted into the edges of lined wrapping cloths. Interestingly these are not all a uniform size, adding more character and personality to the effect. See pages 92–93 for details on making them.

Kileoki is a knot embellishment named after a bird that mates for life. It is used to decorate wedding bojagi as a wish for a long and happy married life for the couple. The *kileoki* knot is made by looping two strips of medium-weight fabric together to form an attractive knot. Made using two contrasting colours, several of these pairs of strips are inserted into the tie of the wrapping cloth. Once the fabric strips have been linked, the edges are drawn together with an elongated cross stitch, using a contrasting thread, to keep them lying flat.

These knots have the potential to be used to join contemporary textile work together. You could change the scale and replace fabric with machine-wrapped cords, ribbons or plastics instead. They could be used to symbolically represent two interdependent ideas.

Decorative jat ssi
(pine nut) table cover.

Khojipgi is a pinching technique, and this raised embroidered outline is usually found on single-layer *jogakbo* made in ramie or hemp fabrics. The fabric is pinched, adding a raised pin tuck. It is often used to create a symbolic shape such as a lotus flower and used as a central motif for a larger carrying cloth. It can be worked in a running stitch or overcasting stitch. I learnt to create a design first on hanji paper and then to transfer this to the fabric by tracing over it with a creaser. The creased lines are then folded and stitched, usually in a matching thread. It is also possible to mark lines freehand or against a ruler.

Lotus leaf covering cloths, with khojipgi *stitched veins.*

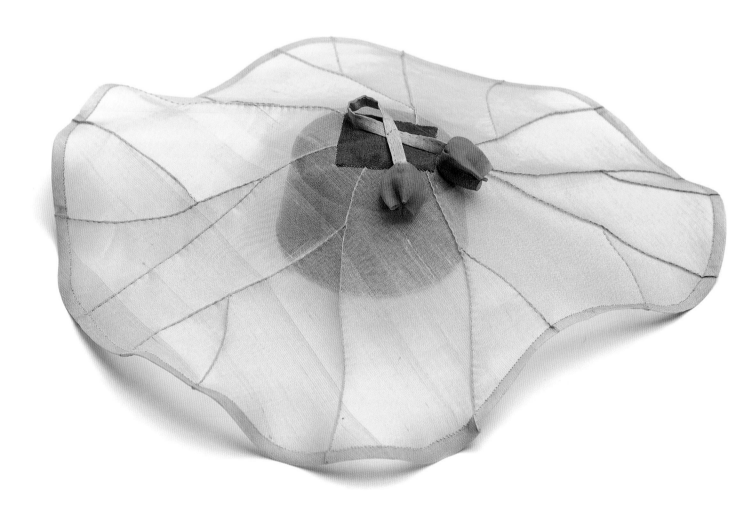

Decorative flower shapes, described to me variously as a tulips or fuchsia flowers, appear on many commercially available bojagi sold to tourists. I have not observed flowers on traditional wrapping cloths but they are nonetheless rather pleasing embellishments that neatly close the ends of cords. The *garakji mae dup* knot is more often added to the ends of cords used as drawstrings.

Tea caddy carrying cloth with decorative flowers.

BAKGI MAE DUP

1 Thread your needle with a strong double thread and make a clean knot at the end. Trim away any loose ends close to the knot. Put to one side. Cut a 5cm (2in) square of fabric and fold the square in half diagonally. Use your fingers to make a crease line in the centre.

2 Place a long bead-headed pin in one corner, close to the edge and parallel to the centre crease line. Place another pin in the opposite corner, pointing in the opposite direction.

3 Roll the first pin between your thumb and index finger, tightly rolling the fabric around the pin shaft.

4 Continue rolling until the pin reaches the centre crease line. Ease the head of the pin outwards as it becomes covered in fabric.

5 Once the roll has reached the centre crease line hold the roll firmly in place while you gently remove the pin. Use the same pin to spear the roll. Repeat steps 3–5 with the other pin.

6 Fold the rolled piece of fabric over at the centre, rolls facing outwards. Hold the two ends together approximately 6mm (¹/4in) below the top folded edge in your left hand (left handers – hold it in your right hand).

7 Pick up your threaded needle and pass it through the two rolled edges facing you. Turn the piece over and pass the needle through the two rolled edges facing you now.

8 Repeat step 7 and then wind the thread several times around the rolled edges, keeping a 6mm (¹/4in) away from the top edge. Pass the needle back and forth through all the layers several times to secure the thread, but do not cut this off.

9 Holding the thread out of the way, trim away the excess fabric as close to where you have wound the thread as possible.

10 Using the thread that is still attached to the bat decoration, pass the needle to the wrong side of the wrapping cloth and come up again through one of the bat wings and take the needle down across the wing on the same side. This will enable you to hide your stitches. Be careful not to pierce the rolls and your stitches will be invisible.

Detail from a two layer bojagi covering cloth made using oQamoQa fabrics. Bat knots used here decoratively to hold the two layers together.

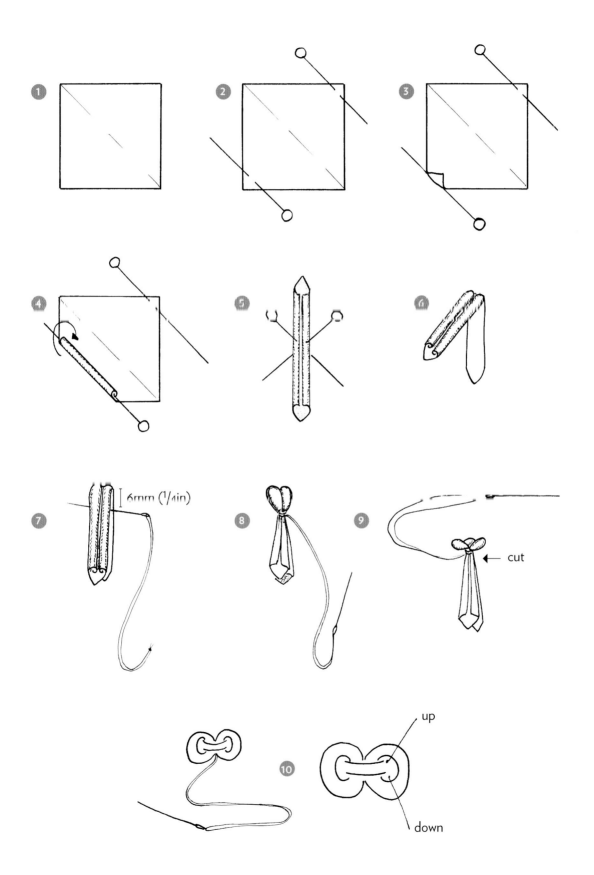

6mm (¼in)

cut

up

down

DUTTAM SANGCHIM AND SETTAM SANGCHIM

These decorative stitches can be worked in groups of two (*duttam*) or three (*settam*) around the edge of a wrapping cloth. Some makers of traditional wrapping cloths like to arrange the same number of groups of stitches on each side of the work to achieve harmony and balance.

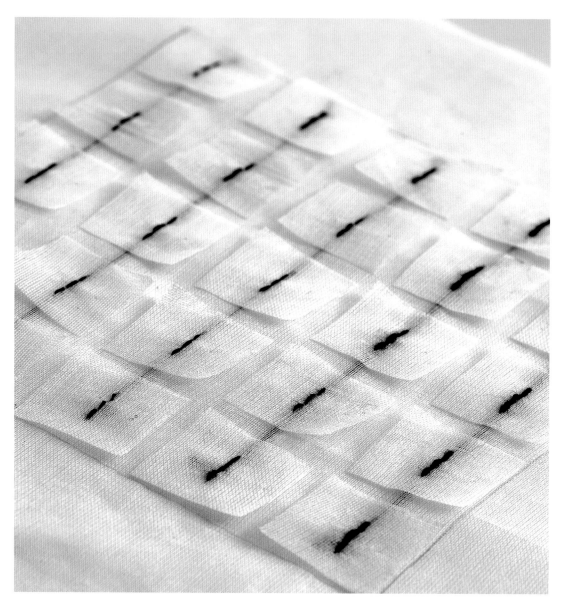

Left: Mark making using groups of settam sangchim (*three stitches*), using different thread thickness on cotton organdie.

Right: Banjitgori (*sewing box*) showing vertical rows of settam sangchim (*three stitches*) used on each side of a panel of khojipgi (*pinching technique*) to hold a border of fabric in place.

1 Thread a needle with a single thread and make a knot at one end. Begin by hiding your knot between the layers of your work. Bring the needle out to the front of the work and sew one backstitch. Your backstitches should go through the back of the piece.

2 Sew a second backstitch. Try to make them exactly the same size.

3 As you sew a third backstitch let your needle travel along the back of the work to begin a new group of three stitches. You will see a loop of thread on the wrong side.

4 Begin another set of three backstitches.

5 Finish your work with a knot and hide this in the layers. With finer fabrics you can pop the knot through the fabric to the wrong side as the fibres will part. For thicker fabrics you will need to take your thread to the wrong side and finish with a knot there.

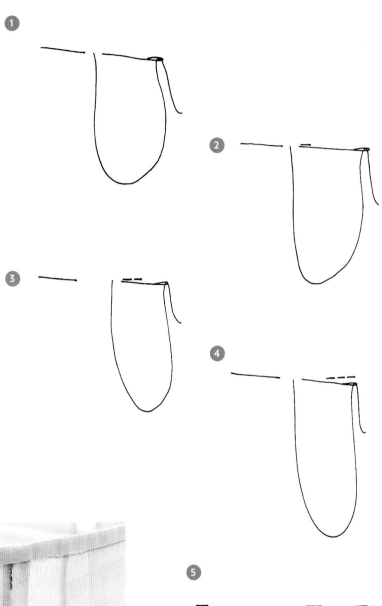

view from the wrong
side of the work

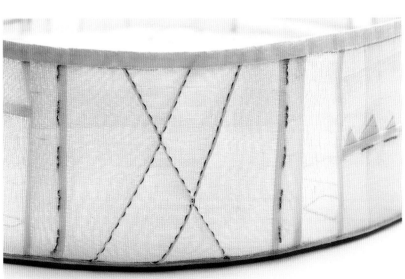

JAT SSI (PINE NUT)

These are traditionally made from different coloured small squares of fabric. They are often inserted into seams and, as well as being symbols of good luck, add an interesting textural effect. They appear to be very similar to prairie points, which are also made by folding and refolding a square of fabric but to form a right-angle point. *Jat ssi* decorative points finish with either a 50- or 60-degree angle.

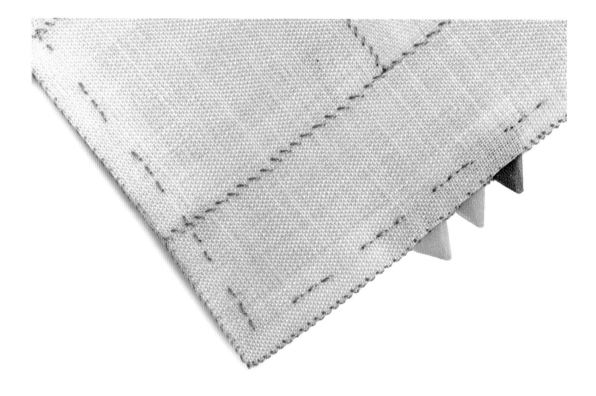

1 Thread a needle with a single thread and set to one side. Cut a 3cm (1¼in) square of fabric. Fold the square in half diagonally to form a triangle. Fold the triangle in half again to find and mark the centre of the folded edge.

2 Using the centre mark as a guide, fold one corner over at the mid-way point of the folded edge.

3 Fold the other corner over the first and even these folds out to create a sharp point at the marked centre of the original folded edge.

4 Take the needle and single thread and stitch a temporary cross to hold the folded edges in place. Make sure this is towards the top of the pine nut. Use a pair of small scissors to trim away the uneven edges at the bottom.

5 Make as many of these as you need and then insert the raw edge of the pine nuts between two layers of fabric. Remove the temporary holding stitches.

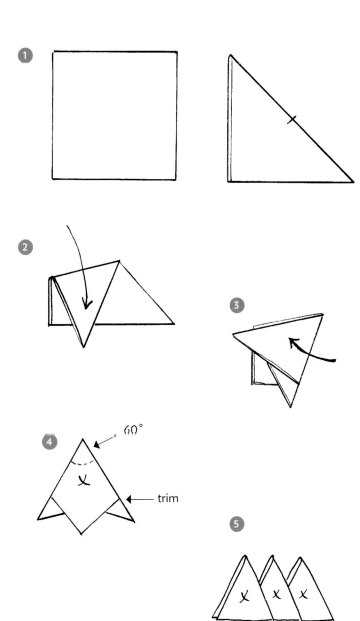

KILEOKI (WEDDING KNOT)

The measurements I have given below are only a guide. I have seen different sized knots formed from different width and length tabs, but all have followed a similar construction method. With regard to the size of fabric strips to cut, I have deliberately given two sets of measurements, one for imperial and one for metric. The two measurements do not convert exactly when marking out the fabric into quarters, so choose to follow either the metric or imperial measurements but don't mix the two.

1 Cut two strips of medium-weight fabric measuring 2 x 12cm (1 x 5in). Thread a needle with medium-weight thread. This can be a silk thread, a single strand of embroidery thread or 30 weight quilting thread. Put a knot on the end. Use a creaser and ruler to mark the centre fold line down the length of each strip of fabric and a 6mm ($^1/_4$in) seam allowance either side of the fold line. Measure from the centre out rather than from the cut edges. This will help with accuracy.

2 Use an iron to press each strip of fabric in half lengthwise.

3 Open the fabric strips out flat again and press the seam allowances towards the centre fold line – they should meet in the middle.

4 Press each fabric strip in half once again along the centre fold line.

5 Bend the first fabric strip in half to form a loop. Hold the two ends together between your thumb and finger towards the base of the strips.

6 Pick up your threaded needle and hide the knot between the folds of the fabric about 6mm ($^1/_4$in) from the base of the strips. Stitch the folded edges together using overlapping cross stitches. Refer to the diagram for how the stitch is formed. Your needle should travel through all four folded edges for each stitch you make. Hold the edges together with your thumb and finger, adjusting them as you work up towards the loop end of the tab. Continue stitching until you reach 2cm ($^3/_4$in) from the looped end.

Banjitgori *(sewing box) panel of* kileoki *(wedding knot) decoration.*

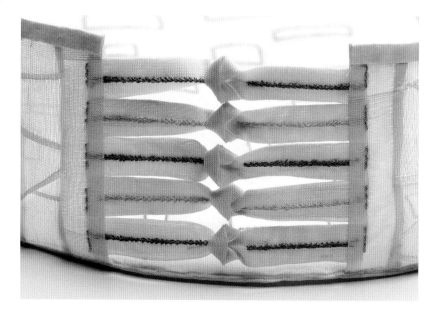

94

7 Finish by taking your needle to the back of the work and make a knot. Hide the end by running it through the folds of fabric. Open out the two sides of the tab and gently press open. Repeat steps 5–7 for the second tab.

8 Thread each tab through the loop of the other with the right sides facing upwards and gently pull the ends in opposite directions.

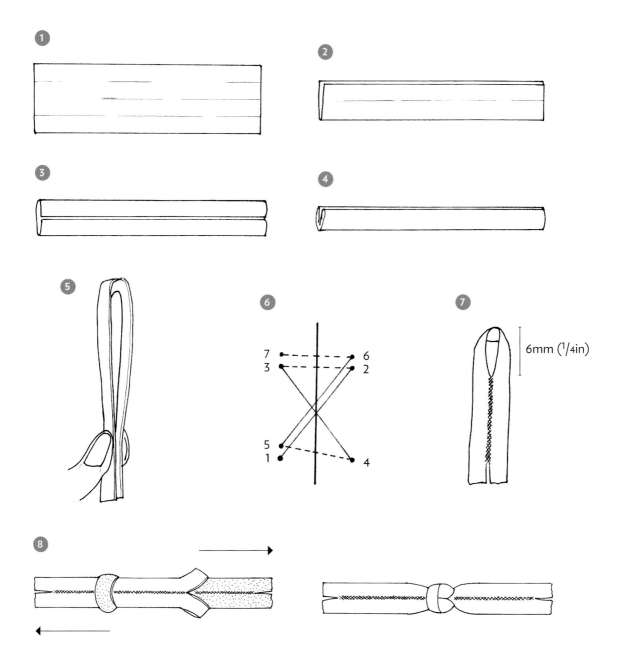

CHAPTER 5

JOGAKBO
OR PIECED
PATCHWORK

Hanbok

Hanbok is the name for traditional Korean costume and its production is intrinsically linked to making bojagi. *Hanbok* clothing is largely cut from rectangular and triangular units. The women's jackets varied in length and shape as the fashions of the period changed. The width and shape of the sleeves of a woman's jackets also varied. Sleeves were cut out in rectangles and stitched together with a curved seam. In some cases the excess fabric was trimmed away but in most cases it was left inside the garment. However, where curved side seams shaped the fabric towards the body, excess would have had to be trimmed away.

Singers wearing traditional hanbok clothes at a festival in Suwon, Korea.

It is worth noting here that when *hanbok* was to be washed it was completely unpicked and flattened out. This explains perhaps why excess fabric was left inside. Collars that touched the neck were covered with a narrow strip of hanji paper folded over the edge. This could be replaced more frequently.

Of course we cannot know for sure where the scraps of fabric used for bojagi came from. Many examples of *jogakbo*, however, do show irregular shaped triangular pieces of fabric, which suggests they were made out of leftover fabric from making garments. Piecing valuable scraps of fabric together to make more fabric follows the ideas of frugality and simplicity advocated by Confucian philosophy.

Most Korean clothes were still being made by hand up until the 1950s. The sewing machine was only introduced to South Korea in the 1930s by the Singer sewing machine company. Singer had long ago hit upon the idea of hire purchase so that even the less wealthy could eventually own one of their machines. Just how common it was to own a sewing machine I do not know, but given that the Second World War followed by the Korean War caused so much disruption and movement of people, it makes sense that they may have been fairly uncommon until the late 1950s.

The Queen *(right) and*
detail (below) by Yoojin Kim.

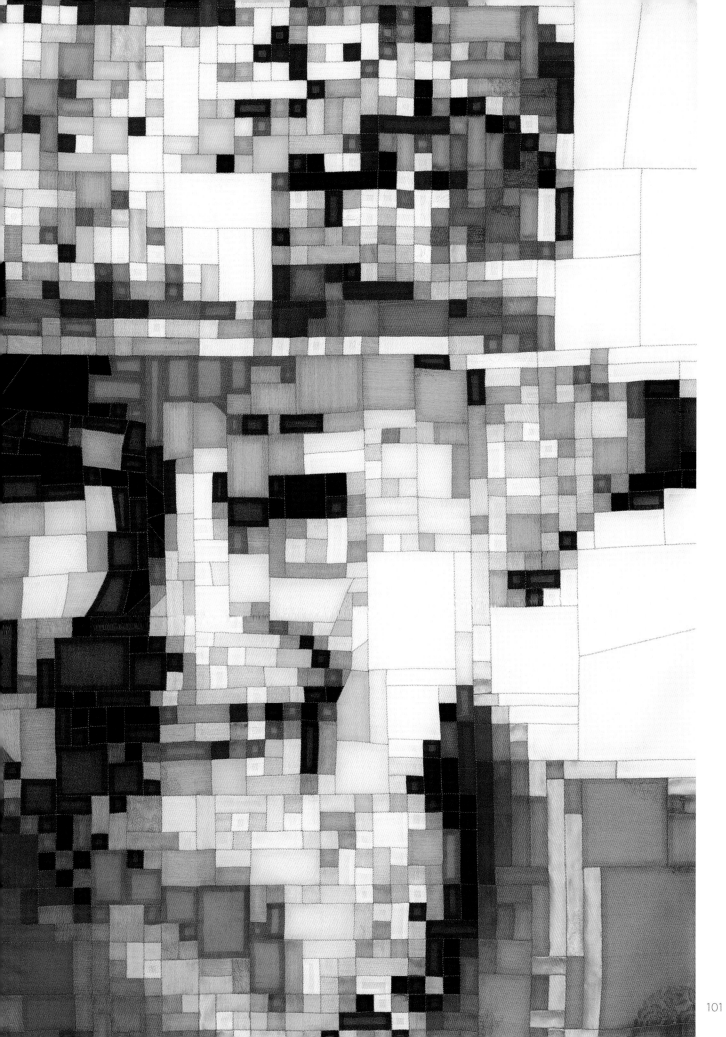

101

Jogakbo

Jogakbo translates as 'small segments' and is often likened by academics to modern abstract art such as that created by Piet Mondrian and Paul Klee. The use of grids in Western art came to prominence in the early 20th century and, as a visual structure, continues to lie at the heart of much contemporary art.

According to Christina Sumner, principal curator of Design and Society at the Powerhouse Museum in Sydney, 'The selection of shapes and the choice of colours were essentially a creative endeavour; with *jogakbo*, however, the fine stitching of the many seams was more akin to prayer, an act of dedication and devotion through which each stitch contributed to the accumulation of blessings in the finished work.'

The process of hand stitching can be meditative when the maker is skilled. Even stitches cannot be achieved by an agitated mind. The makers of *jogakgbo* could have chosen to piece their fabric scraps together with a simple flat seam and running stitch. Instead they used an overcasting stitch that was often worked from the right side of the fabric in a contrasting coloured thread. If the sole purpose had been to make more fabric from leftover scraps the pieces would not have been so artfully put together or indeed cut so small. Dr. Kumja Paik Kim, emeritus curator of Korean Art at the Asian Art Museum of San Francisco, suggests that their work can be compared to the spiritual

Detail from The Queen *by Yoojin Kim. Tiny squares of silk fabric pieced together with a garumsol seam.*

elevation that men aimed for with copying sutras (Buddhist teachings) or painting multiple pictures of Buddhas. The women who made these intricate bojagi must have similarly believed that blessings and good fortune (*pok*) would be accumulated with every additional stitch and piece of fabric added. Their aim, however, would have been to imbue the work with luck for the benefit of the receiver and not themselves.

Mothers, aunts and grandmothers would have made wrapping cloths to give to their daughters who, when married, would often be cut off from their own family. The textiles that went with them remained one way of linking the families together after marriage. With little control over their own lives, women would have had to rely on the hope that their prayers and the symbols of *pok* (good luck) included in the work, would benefit the recipient. The quality of the wrapping cloths that the bride took with her could also help win respect from her new family.

Chequerboard covering cloth.
Squares of sukgosa (fine silk
gauze) pieced together with a
garumsol seam.

Left: Diamond Dots *(2011) by Marian Bijlenga.*
Horsehair, fabric, viscose and machine embroidery
held together in an informal grid of lines that invisibly
link the shapes.

Right: The Screaming Dreams of Flowers *(2018) by*
Jan R Carson. Translucent silk fabrics that are sliced
and seamed in repetitive turns.

Following page: Greyline #1, *152 x 120cm (60 x 47in).*
The line that divides night and day as shadows
lengthen and colours fade. Pieced from hand-dyed silk
organza with French seams, the two layers are held
together with bakgi mae dup *(bat knots).*

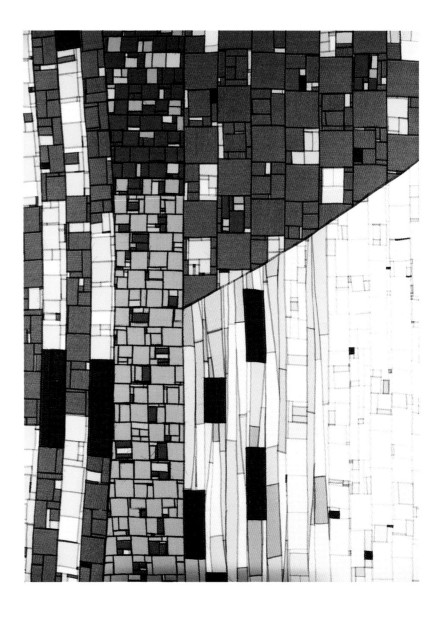

Many surviving *jogakbo* wrapping cloths from
the Choson period appear never to have been
used. Their survival suggests these particular
bojagi were highly valued for the skilfulness of
their makers and were handed down through
the generations. The good wishes and hopes
of a happy life that these wrapping cloths were
imbued with may also have contributed to the
survival of these textiles, providing people with
a tangible link to their families.

Most surviving *jogakbo* date from the second half of the 19th and early 20th centuries, and the
most vibrant examples are made from silk. There are no surviving *jogakbo* found to date that were
used at court. It would seem that they were made only by the *min-bo*, the ordinary people.

The women who created these functional items chose the colours thoughtfully. Making *jogakbo*
required great skill in design, planning the colours and joining the small pieces together carefully.
There is nothing rough or utilitarian about the pieces of work, whether they were made in silk or
ramie fabrics. Those made from asymmetrical pieces can seem to have random arrangements of
colours but in the most accomplished you quickly become aware of a sense of balance and
harmony in the work.

Different types of *jogakbo*

Jogakbo can be divided into several different categories: Those pieced from ramie or hemp, silk *jogakbo* pieced in even-sized squares and triangles in a grid pattern, those that have a central square around which other shapes are arranged, and those pieced in freeform designs.

Those made from silk were lined and were made either to wrap gifts or for covering food. Many have a small tab or knot that was used as a handle to lift them up. Some were lined with oiled paper to protect the cloth from food stains. Some were made entirely of oiled paper and decorated with symbolic shapes cut from coloured paper.

Art-Red 8888 (2016) by So La Lee. Moshi jogakbo, one layer of pieced ramie fabric using ssamsol (fell seam) to join the pieces together.

Mosi jogakbo Larger examples made from ramie and hemp fabrics were not lined. The fabric pieces were joined together by *ssamsol*, a seam that enclosed all the raw edges. Seen against the light, the translucent qualities of the fabric reveal an irregular grid of seams.

Most surviving examples are pieced together using various shades of the same colour. At their most basic, they were made from undyed hemp or ramie. This may have reflected the cost and limited availability of dyes but some do survive in plain reds or blues while others have combined gently muted colours. Some are pieced in an organized way while others are a riot of shapes that seem to defy any planning. These larger pieces often have a pinched good-luck design at the centre.

These larger wrapping cloths were made for utility purposes; wrapping clothing, bedding and for carrying washing and food. Those hung on a wall were thought to repel evil spirits as the open weave of the ramie and hemp fabrics was thought to trap the spirits. Many surviving historical examples show a good deal of wear.

Smaller ramie covering cloths made to cover food are more likely to be lined and pieced with *gamchimjil* (whipstitching).

Jogakbo made from silk fabrics *Jogakbo* made from fine silk fabrics
were pieced using a *garumsol* seam that was pressed open. This type
of work was traditionally lined as the seams on the wrong side were left
raw. Those pieced from regular-shaped units – squares and rectangles
– were often finished by turning in the raw edges and butting them up
before overcasting the edges together. Finishing this way meant there
was no need to 'bag out' the fabric at the end.

Those made from irregular shapes were often finished with a border.
The many different shaped pieces would have had grainlines going in
all different directions along the edges. To achieve a straight edge
would be very challenging. The borders were usually formed by
folding the lining fabric over onto the patchwork front, rather than
adding separate strips of border fabric.

Jasu jogakbo These embroidered, lined wrapping cloths were made
using regular square and triangular units. They were often decorated
with symbolic embroidered images or auspicious letters.

Nemo jogakbo and semo jogakbo Square patterned (*nemo*) and
triangular patterned (*semo*) patchwork. These were mostly pieced
from silk fabrics with the lining used to form the border on the right
side. Decorative stitching held the border in place.

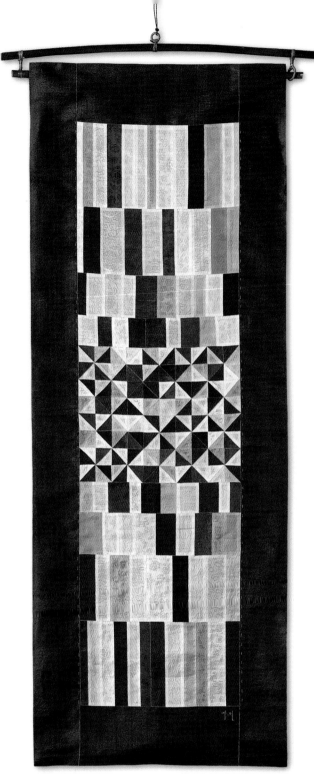

Above: Blue Door *by
Youngmin Lee. Jogakbo
made from geometric
shapes in silk fabrics.*

109

Other designs were made using strips of fabrics or strips arranged around a central square not unlike a log-cabin quilt block. There are many variations and combinations of geometric shapes. Not all are symmetrically arranged.

Honhaphyung jogakbo This is essentially freeform piecing by hand. I have observed that when you look closely at *jogakbo* the pieces are often joined together into regular and irregular units. There is a sense in some of the larger ramie carrying cloths of real organic growth with every shape of leftover fabric pressed into service.

Divided Patchwork (2015) by Magenta Kang (right) and detail (above). The tiny gamchimjil *(whipstitching) join the many hundreds of tiny silk scraps using* garumsol *and contrasting thread.*

Jogakbo pieced from irregular shapes were usually unadorned with embroidery. The beauty of the colours was decoration enough.

Crazy patchwork Crazy patchwork, which was influenced by Eastern design, bears some resemblance to *jogakbo* but is made using different weights of fabric laid down onto a foundation cloth. *Jogakbo* was pieced together. Crazy patchwork was usually highly embellished with fancy embroidery, beads and lace. The imagery used was often drawn from the everyday rather than occupying any symbolic relevance. The fashion for making this type of patchwork enjoyed a relatively short period of time at the latter part of the 19th century, compared to Korean wrapping cloths that were continuously made from as early as the Silla dynasty (57BC–935AD) until the 1950s. Crazy patchwork had no uniformity as to size or use, whereas *jogakbo* were made with a uniformity of scale and for specific functions. They were both, however, made by women who perhaps shared similarities of being excluded from formal education and whose lives were restricted. Both techniques are now valued for their skilful workmanship.

English paper piecing is traditionally pieced in a similar way to *jogakbo* with oversewing used to join the shapes together, but the stitching was not intended to be visible. *Jogakbo* was not pieced over papers and the stitching was often worked in a contrasting thread on the right side of the work, drawing attention to the stitching rather than concealing it.

THE QUILTS OF GEE'S BEND

We can see similarities of composition of improvisational piecing in the quilts of Gee's Bend, Alabama, US, a community cut off from mainstream society by geography and poverty. Thrift drove the women to use what they had to make quilts and through these they expressed their creativity. From used and worn-out clothing they created beautiful bold designs, so that when their work was brought to public attention in 2002 it took the art scene by surprise. The makers of these iconic quilts were not trained artists. They lived isolated lives free from outside influence, much like the women of the Choson dynasty.

When we look at the larger pieces of *jogakbo* pieced from ramie and used to wrap clothing and bedding, the Gee's Bend quilts appear to have a similar process-led approach. To achieve an overall pleasing design, pieces of fabric were arranged and rearranged until the maker was satisfied with the result. Gee's Bend quilters thought like artists, commenting that, after working in the field all day, the difficult part of their day was going back to work on their quilts. We can only guess at what the women of Korea felt about their creative work.

SKETCHES OF *JOGAKBO* VIEWED IN THE COLLECTION OF DR HUH DONG-HWA

I made the following sketches in 2016, when I had the opportunity to view this extensive collection of bojagi during my visit to Korea. Despite not showing colour, you can see the variety in piecing styles.

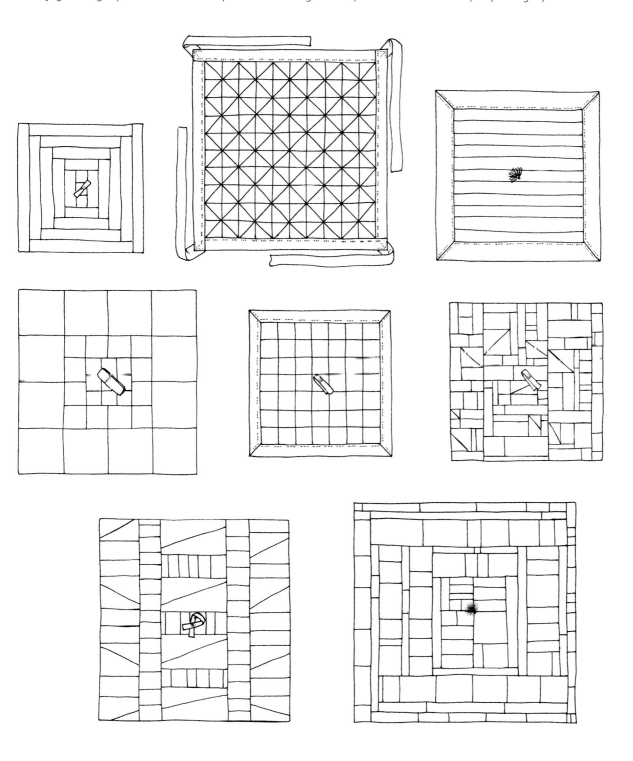

CHAPTER 6

NUBI OR
QUILTING

Nubi and saeksil nubi

Quilted items were made for use in the royal household as well as by ordinary people for use in their daily lives. Quilting was used to produce wrapping cloths to keep food warm or to wrap precious objects, for clothing and bedding, as a protection from the cold, and there is evidence that it was used to make protective padded garments for soldiers to wear.

Many examples of historical clothing, some of which were quilted, were discovered during the 1980s when a large number of ancestral graves in Korea were relocated. These revealed that the people were buried in funeral clothes, with additional clothing packed into the coffin to prevent the body from shifting. Quilted clothing had survived from as early as the mid-Choson period. The excavated artefacts indicate that there was an established tradition of quilting. It may have predated this period but, unlike the Confucian tradition of burial, the previous eras mostly favoured cremation.

Winters in Korea can be very cold and long with temperatures dropping to –20°C in the northern regions, yet rising to 30°C in the summer. This climate makes it highly probable that the use of quilting predates the Choson period.

One theory suggests that quilting developed from the patched robes or *nap-ui* worn by Buddhist monks, whereby discarded fabrics would be stitched and patched together in overlapping layers. Monks were supposed to be humble so that the purchase or wearing of fine clothes was not considered seemly.

①

Unspun cotton fibres (1); mulberry paper twisted into cords (2); cut mulberry paper strips(3); cable knitting needle (4); silk thread (5).

Earlier evidence of quilted items appears in mural paintings in Goguryeo from the 4th to 6th century. *Cheonmado*, a set of saddle flaps made to protect the rider from mud, survive and were made of several layers of birch bark joined together by rows of stitch arranged in a diamond pattern. The *anyok*, a hemp cloth made to sit over the saddle, was made of layers of fabric and stitched in a pattern of squares.

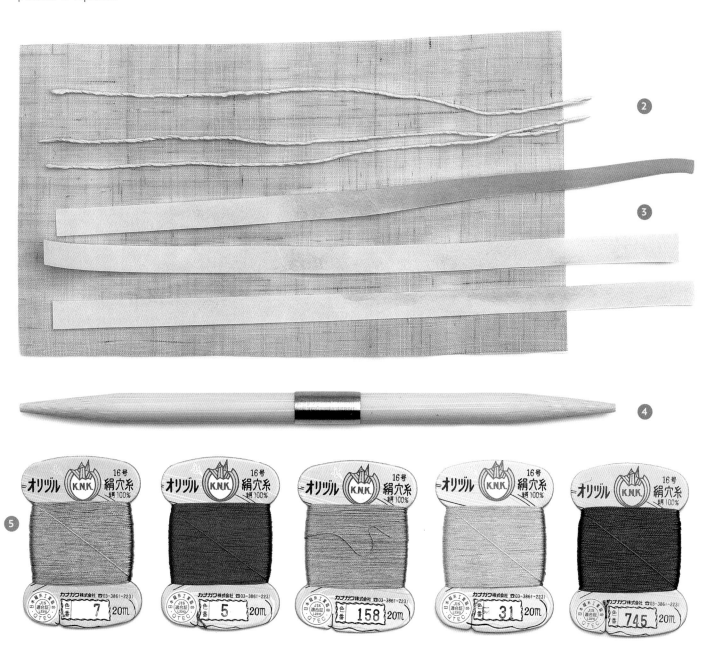

Types of *nubi*

It is possible to see similarities between *nubi* and quilting carried out in the West. The density of waddings that were used varied according to the item's use. The width between the rows of quilting, which was worked in either running or backstitch, also varied depending on how thick the wadding was and what the item was being made for. According to the traditional Korean measuring system, the widths between rows were described as *pun* and *chon*. A *pun* was a gap of approximately 6mm (¼in) and a *chon* was around 5cm (2in).

Traditional Korean children's shoes made by Eun Jin Jeong. Nubi (quilting) sewn in parallel lines, decorated with thread tassels and embroidery.

Historical records describe various types of *nubi*, defining the type by the width of the quilting rows, length of stitches and the type of wadding used. Rows could be closer or wider apart on the same garment, adding extra rows of stitching in different areas. Heavily wadded quilting such as that made for warmth, and outer clothing and bedding could have stitches as frequent as two per centimetre with rows 4–5cm (1½–2in) apart. Finer quilting used for clothing worn in the spring and autumn with only a thin layer of wadding could be worked in rows as close as 3mm (⅛in) with 9 stitches per centimetre (⅜in).

Mulberry paper was sometimes inserted between layers of fabric and in the case of the saddle flaps mentioned on page 117, several layers of birch bark were used as a wadding. Quilting was also carried out without using a separate wadding, whereby stitches were passed through two to five layers of the same material to add reinforcement. This type of quilting is known as *gyeopnubi* (multi-layered quilting), and examples have been found on military jackets.

The quilted bojagi in Dr Huh Dong-hwa's collection vary in size from approximately 50cm (20in) to 180cm (72in) square as well as rectangular shapes. Their uses range from wrapping precious objects to bedcovers, and wrapping cloths used for covering tables and food as well as for wrapping clothes and blankets. They were nearly all made using

straight-line quilting from mostly plain fabrics with matching fabric for ties and details. They could also be more elaborate with embroidery added to them as well.

Wrapping cloths made to wrap rice bowls and to keep food warm would probably have had an additional lining of oiled paper that could be replaced. Ties were attached to the corners of quilted wrapping cloths made from two layers of matching fabric.

Unlike conventional cotton waddings used in modern quilt making, which have a uniform density more like felt, the unspun cotton or silk fibres used for *nubi* are light and lofty, more like cotton wool. The fibres are pulled apart and laid down into thin overlapping layers. Layers could be built up depending on the desired thickness.

The rows of stitching were worked along the straight grain of the fabric. The rows of intended quilting were marked by pulling a single warp thread at measured intervals. This was carried out before the fabrics were sandwiched together.

Traditional child's quilted outfit from the Chojun Textile and Quilt Art Museum, Seoul, Korea.

The grain line is parallel to the selvedge edge, the uncut edge of the fabric. These are the warp threads that are put onto the loom first and are held under tension. This means they have the least amount of stretch. It makes good sense to work lines of quilting along the straight grain as the fabric will remain stable while stitching and be less likely to twist out of shape.

Saeksil nubi or coloured-thread quilting

Saeksil nubi is quilting that uses fine strips of hand-rolled mulberry paper held in narrow channels of curved and geometric patterns worked in backstitch with coloured threads on a plain background. A plain-weave cotton was used with narrow strips of twisted mulberry paper 1–2cm ($^3/_8$–$^3/_4$in) wide, twisted into 1–3mm ($^1/_{16}$–$^1/_8$in) cords. These were used to fill the space between the stitched channels spaced at around 3mm ($^1/_8$in) intervals. The cords were not threaded through the channels but placed in position and the line of stitching worked next to the cord. All the cording was completed before cutting out shapes for a finished item.

This method was used for small items such as tobacco pouches, glasses cases and thimbles designed to help keep objects durable and in shape. This skill may have been lost had it not been for the dedication of Kim Yoon-sun, former Director of the Costume Culture Association and a Professor at Ewha Women's University in Seoul, who dedicated her life to studying and reviving the technique in the 1980s.

Korean items show a resemblance to corded quilting carried out in Europe. The city of Marseille in France has a rich tradition of this type of work, known as *broderie de Marseille*, which was at its peak in the 17th and 18th centuries. Lavish designs were used for all manner of items from clothing to bedcovers. It was worked on a plain white cotton or linen fabric with rows of white running stitch or backstitch in a white thread. The stitched channels were, however, threaded with a narrow white cord applied from the back. Perhaps one of the most well-known early European examples of trapunto or stuffed quilting, where the surface of the fabric has been raised, are the Tristan quilts from 14th century Sicily, one panel of which belongs to the Victoria and Albert museum in London.

Contemporary examples of *saeksil nubi* are often stitched using coloured silk thread on a plain fabric and they are now worked in various patterns and floral designs. Although traditionally worked on plain fabrics, corded quilting over pieced fabrics adds another dimension.

You only need to mark the main structure of the design as all subsequent rows are worked in parallel to these initial lines of stitching.

Contemporary makers have made use of ready-made cords or cotton string to insert between the layers instead of the more time-consuming paper cords. Parallel lines can be stitched on a sewing machine using a piping foot to achieve quicker results. This is referred to as *tongyeong nubi* (machine-stitched quilting). This has lots of versatile possibilities.

Saeksil nubi quilted coaster (left) and detail (below). Plain weave cotton, silk thread and twisted paper cords in a traditional flower design.

SAEKSIL NUBI

This technique uses the wonderful fibrous qualities of mulberry paper made from the inner bark of the mulberry tree. When the paper strips are cut and twisted they form a strong cord. When these cords are inserted between two layers of fabric they remain flexible.

YOU WILL NEED

20 paper strips approx
1.5 x 20cm (½ x 8in)

2 pieces of plain fabric
approx 15cm (6in) square

Fabric marking pencil

Embroidery needle,
size 3 or 4

16 weight silk thread

1 Begin by making around 20 twisted paper cords. Gradually twist the paper into cords between your thumb and finger. A lightweight mulberry paper was traditionally used to make these. Place two pieces of plain fabric wrong sides together. One is the top fabric and the other the base fabric which could be a calico.

2 Mark a line down the centre of the fabric using a fabric marking pencil.

3 Thread a size 3 or 4 embroidery needle with a 16 weight silk thread or similar. Back stitch along this line, starting and finishing with a knot. Keep your stitches small and even. Fold back the top layer of fabric and insert a paper cord that is slightly longer than the length of the fabric. Flip the fabric back over and push the cord tightly against the first row of stitching. You might find it useful to have a large wooden cable (knitting) needle or other blunt-ended pointer to help persuade the cord to say in place. This is especially helpful when you are stitching curved designs.

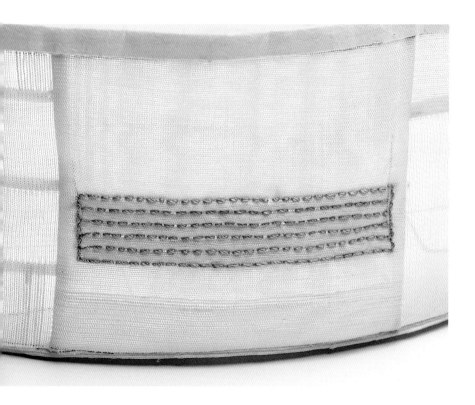

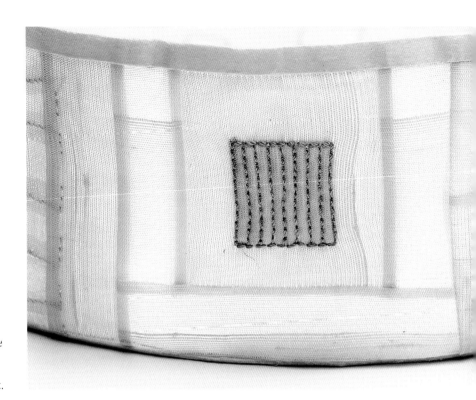

4 Backstitch a second row, creating a channel and trapping the cord between the two rows of stitching. Use your nail as you make your way along the row to keep pushing the cord tightly up against the first row of stitching.

5 Repeat this, building up rows each side of the centre line of stitching. Once the design is complete then it can be treated as one fabric.

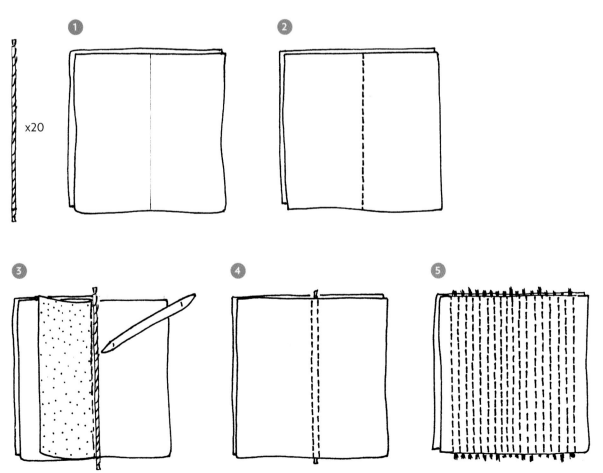

BIBLIOGRAPHY

The Art of Oriental Embroidery: History, Aesthetics and Techniques by Young Yang Chung

Through the Window and Beyond by Lynne Edwards

100 Thimbles in a Box: The Spirit and Beauty of Korean Handicrafts by Debbi Kent and Joan Suwalsky

Nubi: Korean Traditional Quit – Korean Craft and Design Resource Book, Korean Craft and Design Foundation

One Needle One Thread, Miao (Hmong) Embroidery and Fabric Piecework from Guizhou, Chine, by Tomoko Torimaru

Bogaji in Korea Sookmyung Women's University, Seoul, by Jung Hye Ran

Korean Art and Design, Victoria and Albert Musuem 1992 Exhibition Catalogue

Suwon Gybang Art and Craft Institute 2016 Exhibition Catalogue

Bojagi's Simple Elegance By Dr. Huh Dong-hwa

Letters from Joseon, 19th Century Korea Through the Eyes of an American Ambassador's Wife, written and compiled by Robert Neff

The Art of Korea: Highlights from the Collection of San Francisco's Asian Art Museum by Kumja Paik Kim

Highlights from the Korea Collection of Rijksmuseum Volkenkunde by Elmer Veldkamp

Treasures from Korea, Arts and Culture of the Joseon Dynasty 1392-1910, edited by Hyunsoo Woo

Creative Women of Korea, edited by Young-Key Kim Renand, Chapter 8 'A celebration of life, Patchwork and embroidered Bojagi by Unknown Women' by Kumja Paik Kim

Couture Korea, edited by Hyonjeong Kim Han, Exhibition catalogue, San Francisco Asian Art Museum.

Korea the Impossible Country by Daniel Tudor

Fabric for Fashion, The Complete Guide by Clive Hallet and Amanda Johnston

Profusion of Colour: Korean wrapping cloths in the Chosen Dynasty, Asian Art Museum of San Francisco and The Museum of Korean Embroidery, Seoul, 1995

Rapt in Colour: Korean textiles and costumes of the Choson Dynasty, edited by Claire Roberts and Huh Dong-hwa, Powerhouse Museum and The Museum of Korean Embroidery.

A Precious Gift: Nubi by Kim Yoon (Korean Crafts and Design Foundation)

Marseille: the cradle of white corded quilting by Kathryn Berenson

Wrapping and Unwrapping Material Culture: Archaeological and Anthropological Perspectives by Susanna Harris (Editor), Laurence Douny (Editor)

The Journal of the Asian Art Society Volume 20 No. 3 September 2011 *Considering bojagi: traditional and contemporary Korean wrapping cloths* by Christina Sumner

REFERENCES

Dorothy Ko, JaHyun Kim Haboush, Joan R. Pigott, eds., *Women and Confucian Cultures in Premodern China, Korea, and Japan*, Berkeley: California University Press, 2003, p. 143.

Maria, Tulokas, 'The Evolution of Bojagi' in *Surface Design Journal, Summer 2014*, 2014, pp. 16-21, accessed February 12, 2016.

Ten Longevity symbols https://www.philamuseum.org/exhibitions/795.html?page=3

Bojagi wrapping Cloths by Youngmin Lee (Video) www.youngminlee.com

Studio Galli Fine Arts & Crafts Films www.gallifilms.com

SUPPLIERS

Whaleys
www.whaleys-bradford.ltd.uk
Phone: 01274 576718
Fine weight ramie, linen and silk organza, cotton organdie

Art Van Go
www.vycombe-arts.co.uk
Phone: 01438 814946
Cotton organdie, silk organza and fabric dyes

Sew Hot
www.sewhot.co.uk
Phone: 0330 111 3690
Sue Daley #9 Milliners needles
Clover Appliqué needles #9
Extra fine pins

Kemtex educational suppliers
www.kemtex.co.uk
Phone: 01706 831808
Procion dyes

Pongees Silk Showroom
Phone: 02077399130
Coloured silk organza

Jogakbo pieced panel in silk.

INDEX

ACKNOWLEDGEMENTS

I was lucky enough to be introduced to Dr Huh Dong-hwa by Youngmin Lee in 2016 at his flat in Seoul where we spoke about how he came to start collecting bojagi. His collection has been seen in exhibitions around the world and has had huge influence in raising awareness of this wonderful textile tradition. It was with great sadness that I learnt of his death in 2018.

I would like to thank Chunghie Lee who first piqued my interest in bojagi and who introduced me to so many artists. Without her dedication to sharing bojagi through her own work and that of the bi-annual Korean Bojagi Forum the world of textiles would be much poorer.

Thank you to the Quilters Guild of the British Isles who provided me with a bursary to travel to learn more about bojagi from teacher Youngmin Lee who has been a tower of support throughout this process, answering my endless questions and even putting up with me for a whole week in her house.

Thank you to all the textile artists who generously agreed to share images of their work and that demonstrate the diverse way the principles and techniques of bojagi can be interpreted.

I must also thank friends, textile artist and author Elizabeth Betts and dressmaking author and teacher Wendy Ward, who encouraged me to write the book in the first place. Family are often taken for granted but I have always felt their support cheering me on – so thank you too.

PICTURE CREDITS

All photography by Michael Wicks with additional photography as follows:
Pages 14, 52, 53, 84, 98 and 119 supplied by the author. Pages 16, 21, 22, 26, 32 and 109 photographed by Dana Davis, Oakland CA, US; Page 30 photographed by James Thompson; Page 31 photographed by Michael Wyeth. Pages 29 and 71 supplied by Chunghie Lee. Pages 34–35 and 41 supplied by Marielle Huijsman. Page 68–69 supplied by Eun Kyung Suh. Page 104 supplied by Marian Bijlenga. Page 105 supplied by Jan R Carson. Page 108 supplied by So La Lee. Pages 110–111 supplied by Magenta Kang. Page 118 supplied by Eun Jin Jeong.
Page 18: Asian Art Museum of San Francisco, Gift of Mrs. Chung-Hee Kim, 1993.4. Photograph © Asian Art Museum of San Francisco.